The Children's Media
FOUNDATION

children's media
YEARBOOK
2018

EDITED BY

terri langan AND *frances taffinder*

The Children's Media Yearbook is a publication of
The Children's Media Foundation

Director, Greg Childs
Administrator, Jacqui Wells

The Children's Media Foundation
P.O. Box 56614
London W13 0XS

info@thechildrensmediafoundation.org

First published 2018

ISBN 978-0-9575518-9-3

The Children's Media
FOUNDATION

DARRALL MACQUEEN LTD

Thanks to the Children's Media Foundation for another year of essential campaigning & lobbying for children's content in the UK

WELCOME!
FROM THE CHILDREN'S
MEDIA FOUNDATION

GREG CHILDS

—

We're proud to say that this is the sixth edition of the Children's Media Yearbook. To our knowledge there is no similar publication anywhere in the world.

Its continued existence tells us something about the commitment of the children's media industry in the UK to the children's audience. It's produced by the Children's Media Foundation, and edited by one of our brilliant team of volunteers, Terri Langan. Congratulations to Terri on another fantastic read – a snapshot of the children's media year in all its complexity.

Terri is just one of the many people who work tirelessly behind the scenes to further the aims of the Foundation. They are generally from the kids' content industries and they do this because they care … about the quality, range and relevance of the content children and young people receive in this country, and how that affects society as a whole – now and in the future.

These are difficult and complex times. As market conditions have radically altered, platforms proliferated and audience habits shifted,

so practitioners in the UK – across many sectors, from TV, interactive media, games audio, publishing and more – have been not only resilient but smart in adapting to change, building new partnerships, seeking new funding and generally keeping the industry alert and as a result alive.

You can help too. Contact us if you want to get involved: director@ thechildrensmediafoundation.org.

But equally important is having the resources to continue to bring you publications like the Yearbook, public events and regular information about policy and regulation, and the huge task of constant vigilance and advocacy on behalf of the children's audience.

Distributing this book at the Children's Media Conference has been made possible through generous sponsorship from the Authors' Licensing and Collecting Society (ALCS) and independent production company Darrall

Macqueen. By signing up to CMF as a supporter or patron, you can do your bit to ensure we are still around to inform politicians in the CMF-managed All Party Parliamentary Group for Children's Media and the Arts, that we can lobby organisations like Ofcom or the BFI, as well as parliamentarians and ministers, to achieve successes like the creative industries tax incentives, the new Contestable Fund for children's content and potentially a return to regulation of the commercial public service broadcasters to provide more kids' content. All of this is described in more detail in CMF chair Anna Home's article which follows this introduction. And so we can keep up the connections between industry, policy makers and academic researchers – which our Academic Advisory Board helps us achieve.

In the six-year life of the Yearbook, the kids' industry in the UK has shown incredible resilience and adaptability in the face of massive change in the media landscape. As platforms proliferate, funding comes under pressure and audiences shift their allegiances, UK kids' media has risen to the challenge.

A prime mover in this agility has been the Children's Media Conference in Sheffield – and we want to send our congratulations on its 15th anniversary in 2018. CMC is the place the industry informs itself – and makes the connections it needs to navigate change. Once again the Children's Media Foundation is proud to sponsor and produce the key opening Question Time at CMC – "What's Next for UK Kids?" – to which we'll bring politicians, senior policy makers and industry associations.

We hope the session sets the agenda for the Conference and the year ahead. And we hope too that the Yearbook and the CMF can make their contributions to the continued success of the children's media sector in the UK.

Please recommend the book to friends and colleagues. Copies can be downloaded or paperbacks purchased at:

http://www.thechildrensmediafoundation.org/childrens-media-yearbook-2018

And if you are feeling grateful to those hard workers at CMF – why not become a supporter or patron, or possibly affiliate your company for a relatively small donation? http://www.thechildrensmediafoundation.org/support

Greg Childs
Director
The Children's Media Foundation

EDITOR'S INTRODUCTION

TERRI LANGAN

—

This is the third year I've edited the Children's Media Yearbook. A huge thank you to everyone who contributed to the fantastic range of articles.

As ever, policy questions feature in what are complex times for content-makers. We look at Brexit's impact on animation and how tax relief is benefiting children's productions, and CMF chair Anna Home outlines the other key policy issues facing the children's media industry.

Although we are two separate organisations, the Children's Media Foundation tries to reflect the content of the annual Children's Media Conference in the Yearbook each July. This year sees the 15th anniversary of CMC and we hear from regular attendees what the CMC has meant to them, with several articles touching on topics that will be covered at the conference.

Our research section looks at everything from self-image in young girls, to the representation of migrant children in children's media, and we have news of a major CMF research programme studying children and virtual reality.

More generally, there are articles ranging from the representation of LGBT storylines in children's TV, to the question of how to discuss relationships and sex education in the media for kids. Similarly sensitive is the issue of how to acknowledge that the world children live in isn't perfect, without dumping our fears and worries on them through the entertainment they watch.

Each year we see the focus on digital grow and in this Yearbook we have a whole section devoted to it. We see articles on voice technology, children's safety online and the all-important responsibilities for policing inappropriate content online.

And we congratulate some children's brands that are celebrating big birthdays this year: *Paddington*, *Grange Hill*, *Blue Peter* and the *Beano*.

We hope you enjoy reading what we have compiled as our "snapshot" of children's media in 2018. If you would like to submit an article or research for the 2019 Yearbook, contact me at: yearbook@thechildrensmediafoundation.org.

THE CHILDREN'S MEDIA FOUNDATION YEAR

ANNA HOME

—

It has been a year of consultation, meetings and debate, and as I write this in June, of very few definitive outcomes – yet.

There were three main policy areas with which the Children's Media Foundation (CMF) was concerned, two of which were highlighted in the CMF sponsored Question Time session at CMC last July and will no doubt emerge again as issues in the Question Time "What's Next for UK Kids?" in CMC 2018, once again produced and sponsored by CMF. They were:

1. The role of Ofcom in the regulation of children's content on the BBC, which is inevitably closely related to the potential re-introduction of content quotas for the commercial public service broadcasters (ITV, Channel 4 and Channel 5).
2. The planning for the pilot Public Service Broadcasting Contestable Production Fund.
3. The question of internet safety for children and teens, and possible

regulation of social media, which has gathered momentum during the year.

CMF has been very involved in all these questions.

In the last Yearbook we reported that, due to a timely intervention in the Digital Economy Bill, Baroness Benjamin and the producers' association, Pact, had achieved a government-supported amendment, which in its inevitably diluted form meant that Ofcom was now required to consider whether the time and conditions were right to impose regulations on commercial public service broadcasters to ensure they carried and potentially commissioned more children's content.

Ofcom has begun this work by initiating one of its periodic reviews of children's television. In 2007, Ofcom's Children's Television Review revealed the extent to which commissioning of children's programmes in the UK had decreased, despite the rise in BBC commissioning related to the launch of the new CBeebies and CBBC channels. ITV had already significantly reduced spend, and Channel 4 had ceased to commission children's television. However, at the time, and despite the astonishing statistic that only 1% of the content watched by British children was a first run UK-produced origination, Ofcom was powerless to intervene. In the 2003 Broadcasting Act, children's television had been relegated from the mandatory Tier 2 status to Tier 3, which meant that the regulator was charged with ensuring that there was sufficient provision of children's content from the PSBs "taken together" – and that included the BBC.

Ten years on, Ofcom are conducting a Children's Review once again. In January 2018 CMF responded to the Ofcom consultation on that Review, along with other bodies, including the commercial PSBs. Ofcom will use these responses, plus their own research and information from audience surveys and external research, to consider the "health" of the children's television ecosystem and whether children in Britain are doing well for content – including locally relevant and age-appropriate content across all ages – or whether they are being short-changed.

CMF agreed there was a need for some more research into what kinds of content were required and which audiences were under-served. But in our response we also reiterated the position we have taken since 2007, that there is "market failure", so the

powers granted to Ofcom in the Digital Economy Act provide a real window of opportunity to regulate the commercial PSBs, and redress the balance. In April, we had a follow-up meeting to discuss the timetable for decision-making. Since then Ofcom has been gathering research, conducting industry round-tables, to which we have contributed, and their final report and recommendations are due later this summer.

The Contestable Fund pilot, originally proposed by former Culture Secretary, John Whittingdale, was a policy the Department of Culture, Media and Sport consulted on through 2017 and their decision on the broad structure of the plan was formally announced in December by the then Secretary of State, Matt Hancock. The commitment that the Fund would still be financed to the tune of £60 million over three years, as a pilot scheme, and would be dedicated to content for children and young people, was welcomed by CMF and other interested parties such as Pact and Animation UK. This was a particular success for CMF lobbying, as previously a variety of under-served genres had been under consideration for the Fund. The move to focus on content for young people was exactly what the CMF had suggested would be reasonable for a pilot scheme – focusing on a single audience so that it could be more efficiently assessed, and not spread too thinly, while serving the audience which was the most at risk from market failure.

At the same time the basic structure of the Fund was laid out, including that the further work on detail would be undertaken in collaboration with the British Film Institute (BFI) which was also identified as the organisation best equipped to run the pilot. Work is continuing, led at the BFI by the director of the Film Finance Fund, Ben Roberts, and from our conversations with DCMS officials and the BFI, it's clear that the plans will be finalised before the end of 2018, with the Fund in operation by April 2019. They have also made it clear that the Fund will be targeted at public service content intended for dissemination on free-to-air platforms, either broadcast or on-demand and while co-investment might come from other parties, like the new VoD services (as CMF has suggested), there will have to be a public service outlet for the content attached to each project the Fund supports.

CMF's role in all these discussions has been to advocate for the children's audience, while supporting the children's media industry to achieve the funding it needs to increase the provision of quality, varied and relevant UK-produced content for British kids, and to keep the discussions as open and public as possible. To that end we staged another of our public meetings in January 2018, chaired by senior journalist and broadcaster Stewart Purvis, in which the audience and industry perspectives were discussed in relation to both the future of regulation and the Contestable Fund – as they clearly go hand-in-hand. At the meeting, Magnus Brooke from ITV Policy was honest and forthright about ITV's opposition to regulation and the complexities of operating an intervention fund so that it is of real benefit to the

market and does not bring collateral damage was discussed in some detail. All these issues were discussed again in May at a very well attended event with the title: "The Future of Children's Television", held in Westminster under the auspices of the All Party Parliamentary Group (APPG) for Children's Media and the Arts and the International Broadcasting Trust.

Ben Roberts, Magnus Brooke and Simon Terrington from Ofcom will all be panelists in the CMF Question Time at the Children's Media Conference 2018. Through the work of CMF's dedicated lobbyist, Jayne Kirkham, we will also welcome the deputy leader of the Labour Party, Tom Watson, who heads up the Culture portfolio for the Opposition and was a founder member of the APPG which Jayne runs on behalf of CMF.

The question of how safe the internet and in particular social media websites and apps are for the younger audience has been simmering amongst parents and concerned academics for some years. There are many issues, including grooming, cyber bullying, peer and image pressure, how privacy is handled, social media "addiction", concerns about screen time – especially in relation to playing games, the effectiveness of age verification, parental controls and ease of use, and media literacy amongst children and their parents to equip them to deal with some of the above. The interests of children and teens are well represented by bodies researching and campaigning in this field including Children's England, NSPCC, 5Rights and many more.

For some years CMF has focused on

the responsibilities of the social media platforms for the children that use them – in particular the many thousands who are signed up to YouTube, Facebook and other social apps before the age of 13, which is the legal requirement according to the US COPPA regulations. We have tried to persuade the big social media players to put less faith in their algorithms, put manual moderation in place to protect children from inappropriate content, improve their parental controls and make them more user-friendly and admit that they are in fact publishers rather than just platforms, and as such need to take responsibility for the content they disseminate.

While the Digital Economy Act brought about an age-verification system for legal pornography sites, there was little progress on the less obvious issues – such as the proximity of inappropriate content to children's favourite brands and characters. The House of Lords launched an Enquiry, to which CMF contributed; government consulted on its Safer Internet Strategy and we responded. But it was when politicians began to discover the influence social media was having on the results of elections – particularly when manipulated – and the press began to uncover bad news stories of upset parents whose toddlers had been confronted with disturbing material online, that the current storm broke over the social media sites. The warnings we had been giving for some years became a reality and "What's good for kids is good for business" is something these sites are now learning the hard way. The CMF believes sites such as Facebook and YouTube should be family

friendly by default – with adult material in "walled gardens" rather than the other way around. We pressed the sites to self-regulate, but they didn't take the action needed. Now governments, not least our own, are talking about going further and CMF is supportive of some form of regulation to ensure that sites that generate large revenues among hundreds of millions of users recognise, respect and provide for the children amongst their users – while we continue to support improved media literacy as a fundamental right of children and their parents.

Once again the Internet Safety Strategy is still "under construction" but with the public pressure and press interest, there will almost inevitably be change ahead.

So, it's been a year of slow progress, but with much more on the horizon, as the possibility of regulation, the imminent reality of the Contestable Fund and the prospect of government regulation of the internet all loom large.

To quote this year's Children's Media Conference theme – "What's Next" for the CMF? More work on all of the above to ensure that the children's audience in the UK is well served, with well-resourced content, from a variety of sources, in a variety of genres and aimed at a wide range of the audience age-groups.

Come along to "What's Next for UK Kids" Question Time at the CMC to debate the issues and hear what the policy makers have to say. And of course you could back us all year round by becoming a supporter or patron. ○

15 YEARS:

THE CHILDREN'S MEDIA CONFERENCE

KAY BENBOW

As I head to Sheffield for this year's Children's Media Conference, I reflect on why this gathering is so special for me, having attended almost every year since it began as Showcomotion in 2004. The city has a special place in my heart as Sheffield is where my parents met, set up their first home and where I was born.

I love returning to the city where my dad had such a wonderful time at the university and where my parents made lifelong friends. My feelings are similar. The children's community is very special – a close-knit group who, despite being in competition with one another, have a common cause in creating the best possible content for the next generation. We all know how much this audience matter and how much they should be inspired as they grow, develop and navigate a world that can be confusing and frightening as well as fascinating and beautiful.

Having spent over 25 years in children's programming, I have also made lifelong friends and worked with so many incredibly talented people. As controller of CBeebies, I spoke at the commissioning session every year for seven years, asking the production community to develop a rich and diverse range of content for our very youngest viewers. Without fail they always delivered, surprising and delighting the audience with terrific television, interactive content, radio, apps and more. One memorable moment was when I asked for drama on CBeebies. I was met with some surprised faces but, a year later, I was able to commission the delightful *Katie Morag* and the incredibly popular *Topsy and Tim*, with *Jamillah and Aladdin* and *Apple Tree House* continuing the successful trend. It is

Kay Benbow taking one-to-one meetings at CMC 2013

thanks to the irrepressible community in the UK children's industry that the CBeebies audience has an amazing range of shows across all genres to watch, engage with and learn from, all of which strive to be diverse and inclusive, reflecting the lives of children across the UK.

This year, the theme of "What's Next?" is apt for me now that I am attending as an independent, freelance member of the children's production community. I look forward to catching up with friends and making new connections. I am delighted to be participating in the SkillBuilder session, as I remain committed to nurturing and supporting new talent who want to build a career serving our youngest viewers. We need the next generation of content creators to ignite the imaginations and inspire the dreams of the next generation of viewers and media consumers... ○

ANGELA SALT

Ten years ago, I took a lone, fateful train to the future I hadn't dared imagine for myself. Kylie's "Locomotion" was stuck in my head because I was heading to (what was then known as) the Showcomotion Children's Media Conference.

I wore a *lucky* necklace that said "Super" but was feeling far from it. I was very apprehensive. I'd suffered severe, life-limiting agoraphobia in my twenties and this was the first time I'd travelled independently and stayed away from home in a hotel on my own for a very long time. Added to the anxiety of being away in a strange, faraway place (Sheffield!) was the prospect of leaving my three young children behind (I'd taken a long break from my former career as a freelance editorial illustrator, part-time university tutor and Scholastic author to be a stay-at-home mum) and turning up somewhere daunting where I didn't know *anybody*. Not. One. Soul.

But that was 2008 BCP. Before communal pizza – the now legendary Pizza Express supper where it's impossible to not know anyone by the end of the evening! The CMC was and is a great place to find your feet and meet people who share a love and passion for children's media in all its forms and facets. Little did I know in 2008 just how many amazing, interesting, diverse, clever, encouraging and LOVELY people I would start to get to know... In ten years, thanks to the CMC, I can say with certainty that I've made some great friends for life. I've found ace international colleagues to collaborate and work with on fulfilling projects, including developing an original show I created, *Bear, Bud & Boo*, with Technicolor and Brown Bag Films.

I'm now delighted to be represented as a writer by one of the top international agents in the business, LA-based Annette van Duren, and I'm currently writing for clients in the US, China, Korea and the UK. In ten years, I've gone from reading *Curious George* board books to my children to writing TV episodes on seasons 12/13 for Universal Animation Studios – something I never imagined that I'd be doing. But that's where the solid support and boundless inspiration of the CMC gets you! I feel very fortunate to have made hundreds and hundreds of connections with talented and inspiring people in the wonderful, international, *sociable* world of children's media drawn together and united by the conference. There is something special about the kinship and camaraderie the CMC actively promotes and this is underpinned by a strong sense of shared responsibility and the urge to do the very best creative work for children and young people around the world.

Looking back now, I'm marvelling at that lone, nervous train journey to "Sheffy" which led me to further-flung and fun children's media adventures in Dublin, Cannes, Toulouse, New York, Miami and Beijing (amongst other places), conquering a severe fear of flying along the way. I am proud to have been an ambassador for the CMC at MIPTV and to be a regular returning member of the UK@ KIDSCREEN delegation. I am so utterly grateful that the CMC opened my eyes, my mind and my world in ways that have made a dramatic difference to my life and helped me to find a fulfilling career as an international content creator, creative consultant and writer.

Over the years, I have learned and honed new skills through the CMC, attending Co-production workshops, How To Pitch workshops and Writers' Workshops. I've been thrown to the "Dragons" in the popular "Put Your Money Where Your Mouth Is" session. I've relished the opportunity to meet potential new partners and clients at the superbly managed International Exchange. I've joined the Manimation steering group to help shape the growing CMC one-day event from the perspective of a northwest-based writer. I've found brilliant, supportive and encouraging mentors (which I believe is a key to developing in any field) and I'm glad that I've had the opportunity to give back what I've learned so far – and continue to learn – speaking on panels to encourage other independents and newbies. My eldest daughter, Marlin, who was just ten years old when I first started attending the CMC, has been a regular CMC volunteer for the past few years and I can see how the conference is now giving her an opportunity to grow and explore future career prospects. On a break while transferring university courses, she is currently happily working for Hoho Entertainment in London. I'm proud of her and delighted to see a "second generation" opportunity stemming from the CMC.

The CMC has given me so much to be thankful for and year on year I look forward to it immensely. As an independent, it's a valuable opportunity to soak up and review current thinking, trends and developments; to be inspired by excellent speakers of the calibre of Frank Cottrell Boyce, Henry Winkler, Lemn Sissay, Jess Thom and this year, Michael Rosen.

Maybe, in 2018, I need a new Kylie earworm travelling to The CMC...?! "I don't ever wanna stop / I'm gonna give it all I've got" from *Dancing* on her latest LP, *Golden*. See, there's something else that the CMC has given me and Fun Crew, the company I co-own with Stuart Harrison. The chance to co-host and DJ the official CMC party, Fun CMC, for all registered delegates. Believe me, it's a complete joyous turnaround for a former lone agoraphobe to greet hundreds of conference partygoers arriving at the party and help behind the scenes to ensure that everyone has a great night out! It's my way of extending and paying forward the very warm welcome I was given as a newbie ten years ago.

Thank you to Greg, Kathy, Jacqui and all the lovely people at CMC for *everything*. ○

KATH SHACKLETON

Gosh – I've been looking through the archive and I've been coming to the Children's Media Conference for ten years now. How time flies!

From just popping down the road from West Yorkshire to South Yorkshire, the conference has opened up a world of new possibilities in developing my skills, ideas and connections as an animation producer.

This year, my studio Fettle Animation is six years old – hooray! We're kicking off our third commission for BBC Learning on a BBC Bitesize project and have a range of clients across the broadcast, government, charity and commercial sectors. We've done lots of short form work and are developing our own IP and ideas for longer series work.

I sit in a studio with a shiny trophy cabinet, which fills me with pride at all that we have achieved here at Fettle. We have a Japan Prize, a Sandford St Martin Children's Award, the SLA Information Book Award and two Royal Television Society Awards plus two BAFTA nominations and a British Animation Awards nomination. The connections I made for all of these all started at the Children's Media Conference.

When I first came to the conference, it was still called Showcomotion, and I stood nervously on the edge of the room. I soon realised that here was a place you could meet people quickly, ask questions and get lots of answers. I'm the one you will always find with my hand up, asking the panel "What about animation?".

I've seized all the opportunities I can from this marvellous conference on my doorstep. I've produced three sets of animated conference idents, been a session producer and a blogger. I've enjoyed these opportunities to reflect on the business we are in and give something back.

The Children's Media Conference has also started many travel adventures – from trips to London for Animation Exchange and London Book Fair events, to my first MIPJunior in Cannes, to Kidscreen in Miami. I've been grateful for the support and connections it has given me.

The workshops have also been great. I remember my first ever pitching workshop – we were given just an hour to refine our pitches.

Suddenly a panel appeared with Disney, BBC and ITV execs – gulp! Many of us in that session went on to work with the people on that panel, so tiny acorns really can grow into mighty oaks!

It's quite tough running an animation company right now. Competition is fierce and you have to be agile and adapt well to change if you are to survive and keep yourself healthy in mind and spirit!

Coming to a conference like this, you keep up to date with trends and opportunities and meet friendly and approachable senior movers and shakers in the business.

I've also gained support from colleagues in the same boat, inspiration from others at different stages on their business journeys, lots of encouragement and a chance to hatch new ideas and collaborations.

It's also great to enjoy a much needed few days away from the office, with a laugh, a few beers and chance to strut my funky moves on the dancefloor!

Here's to the next 15 years!
Thank you, CMC! ○

Zane Whittingham Fettle Animation

THE IMPORTANCE OF THE CREATIVE SECTOR TAX RELIEFS FOR CHILDREN'S CONTENT

ANNA MANSI

—

The UK government's creative sector tax reliefs have been a huge success story for the creative industries.

Widening the scope beyond the film tax relief to include tax reliefs for high-end television, animation television, children's television and video games has been a positive move for the children's screen sectors. It has provided much needed finance and support for children's content at a time when this sector was beginning to see a decline.

The government's film policy review in 2011 acknowledged the need for more content aimed at young audiences.

The introduction of the animation television tax relief in 2013 highlighted the breadth of the talent working in UK animation and the opportunity to create more content for UK audiences which could also be exported to international markets. The majority of the applications we have seen for certification at the BFI have been for content aimed at young audiences from pre-school upwards. These programmes provide inclusive and educational storylines and representations that support and develop young minds.

However, the film and animation tax reliefs alone could not support all children's content, and live action children's television content was missing out on a vital financial incentive. (Feature films for young audiences could clearly access the film tax relief.) Credit must be given to the Producers Alliance for Cinema and Television (Pact) and the Children's Media Foundation, who supported and demonstrated the need for a tax relief aimed solely at children's television content. The subsequent children's television tax relief was introduced in 2015. As the first point of contact for the creative sector tax reliefs, we have seen a steady stream of applications for children's television programmes aimed at pre-school children up to 15-year-olds, and there has been a year-on-year increase in the number of programmes that have applied and been awarded certification as British productions. This has primarily been under the cultural test. The total spend on the UK children's TV productions with final certification has reflected this rise and has also grown year-on-year. This increase is partly due to publicising the incentive and consequently raised awareness of the tax relief process.

Significantly, our Research and Statistics Unit (RSU) is able to track the number of applications we receive and look at the data and trends around the reliefs. This invaluable information is digested and used in the BFI's annual Statistical Yearbook, which provides a comprehensive overview of the UK's screen sectors. The data we receive is vital to understand the take-up and impact, and how it benefits the creative sectors both economically and culturally.

To this end, the BFI Certification Unit, in partnership with Pact, Animation UK and key stakeholders, has maintained a regular communications, marketing and promotion strategy to promote the animation programme and children's television tax reliefs at conferences, roadshows and events across the UK and internationally. In addition, since the introduction of the animation tax relief in 2013 and the children's television tax relief in 2015, we have also run a BFI-led Animation Day and seminar and three children's television seminars in Manchester and London. These events not only help to promote the tax reliefs but also focus on the importance of the Creative Skillset Skills Investment Fund (SIF) contributions and diverse inclusivity in creating content.

It has been very important to us to have built a strong and valued relationship with the Children's Media Conference; to have been invited to take part in panels and take meetings with delegates at the conference since 2013 and at the CMC's Manimation events in Manchester – providing advice and guidance on how the tax reliefs work and how they provide financial assistance to make great British content for young audiences. This year, we are delighted that the Certification Unit's regular attendees at CMC, Chris Halliday and Andy Wright, were invited to curate an entire panel session on the topic with experts from the BFI and HMRC, and producers giving an overview of how to qualify, how to claim and how the benefits work in practice.

This indicates the importance of the tax incentives to the children's media industry in the UK and the BFI Certification Unit's continued aim to ensure that every company and project with the right to apply knows that it can do so, and how to achieve the support. ○

THE STATE OF ANIMATION PRODUCTION IN THE UK, 2018

PHIL DOBREE

———

In the UK, we have always been known for our creative excellence. In the last 15 years we have become global leaders in the rapidly growing field of visual effects (VFX) and animation production. We're great at marrying technology and creativity.

Many companies, including Jellyfish, have flourished on the back of work flooding in to the UK with the help of tax credits. Although these financial incentives have, in many cases, proved critical in securing the work, it is our ability to excel at delivering work of a consistently high standard that has helped the UK emerge as a global leader. We have assembled the very best artists and technicians, mixing UK talent with the best from the EU/EEA and the rest of the world. Like any business where skills are at a premium, the ability and requirement to access this talent quickly and easily is critical in helping us maintain our enviable position. The cultural diversity which different nationalities and life experiences bring to any creative workplace enhances our ability to find truly innovative approaches to everything we do. This diversity of talent creates a hive of ideas,

skills and solutions that makes working in this business so special. Jellyfish is typical of most UK animation businesses in terms of the proportions of nationalities we hire. With a staff approaching 200, 50% of our artists are from the UK, 40% from the EU or EEA and 10% from the RoW.

Last year, Jellyfish worked on three of the twelve children's animation series being produced in the UK. To continue to produce top-rated shows like *Dennis and Gnasher: Unleashed*, *Bitz and Bob* and *Floogals*, we need to be able to access talent fast, easily and cost-effectively. We worked extremely hard to find the best animators and technicians globally to deliver our ambition on these shows. This meant utilising all our recruitment channels across the EU and UK, using our relationships with colleges and communities in Spain, Italy, Germany and France amongst others. At its height we needed to recruit more than 100 artists in under six months. This would have been impossible without access to this EU talent pool and we would have been forced to set up studios in territories where we could recruit the required teams easily.

Brexit is clearly a threat to our business in the UK, and not just because there is a shortage of homegrown talent. We rely on the very best talent from all corners of the globe, particularly the EU, because of the diversity, creative talent and knowledge this brings us. If this easy access to talent is switched off, the industry is in danger of shrinking very fast. Not only will it take a generation to improve and grow our domestic talent base, but the gap left by the diversity, experience and knowledge a truly global workforce brings would adversely affect our competitiveness and excellence. At Animation UK, the UK Screen Association and The Creative Industries Federation, we've been working hard to try to ensure that this cliff edge doesn't happen. These organisations have emphasised the need for rapid and inexpensive visa access, particularly for freelancers on whom the industry relies. For some time we've focused on training and education for young people in specific skill areas where we know there are shortages. There is no lack of courses or graduates from colleges and universities in the UK; the issue has predominantly been one of quality not quantity.

In my opinion, it is imperative that companies continue to engage as much as possible with our educational institutions in the UK to help them understand what the industry needs. This means establishing centres of excellence where courses are not under pressure to recruit students to fulfil quotas and secure funding, often at the expense of ability and dedication or commitment from students. Alumni from institutions such as Animation Workshop

Bitz & Bob

(Denmark), Filmakadamie (Germany), Gobelins and ESMA (France) are highly rated globally and most of their graduates gain employment with relative ease. Filling quotas to gain funding makes this aspiration difficult to achieve in the UK. These courses in the EU attract undergraduates from around the world, which again adds to the cultural and creative diversity this brings to the courses.

With the advent of Brexit, we need to ensure that courses in the UK continue to attract the very best students both locally and further afield. However, there is a concern that universities will be under even more pressure if this pool of potential students shrinks dramatically because of visa restrictions.

It is only relatively recently that we fought hard to bring animation production back to the UK by the introduction of tax incentives. This made a significant difference to many companies making animation in the UK, and the industry has picked up significantly as a result. Whilst we now have another threat to contend with, I believe that with the strong base we have rebuilt in the UK, we're in a good position to protect what the industry has worked so hard to achieve. We don't want to go back to the position of creating ideas in the UK only to get them executed elsewhere. We need to provide employment to future generations of talented animators and artists, and to do this we need to remain leaders in animation production, not just creative ideas.

To maintain our access to the very best talent, Jellyfish has made strides to allow artists to work for us wherever they are located by creating a secure cloud-based network. Our studios at the Oval in South London are virtual, which means all our computers are in an offsite colocation. This demonstrates the ease with which we can set up a "virtual studio", wherever the talent resides.

Although we have embraced these innovations in technology, I still believe that to achieve the best work it is important to have people in one location, not split across territories or continents. I want Jellyfish to be part of a thriving UK animation business and this means conversely engaging with the very best talent across the world and bringing them to the UK because this is where the best work is made. It is economically damaging to prevent talent coming here and having to move production to where we can access talent. My fear is, should we have to resort to such measures, the industry will once again shrink. In the same way we shouldn't have to chase tax incentives in other territories to build our studios, nor should we have to do this to access talent. ⊙

THE GOOD, THE BAD AND THE UGLY – THE DIGITAL YEAR

JOHN KENT

—

What with Logan Paul filming in Japan's suicide forest, revelations that smart devices could be listening to you[1], Peppa found to have nobbled her dad and You Tube admitting that its kids' app is unmoderated, it's been a busy year for kids in the digital world.

This has been the year when users, perhaps parents especially, have begun to expect the same standards and values in the digital world as in the real world – and have often been surprised that they don't exist.

It's encouraging that these issues are entering mainstream debate, and it's about time that discussion of internet safety moved on from alarmist proclamations about screen time. But the ongoing, heightening debate around the internet, and particularly the power of the algorithm, usually conflates a series of distinct problems.

In the children's sector, perhaps the biggest tremors have been caused by the stories exploring whether You Tube is a safe environment for kids, the big platforms' reliance on algorithms and AI to curate and moderate content, and the extent of the "YouTube Poop" bootleg videos featuring well known children's characters participating in very adult activities[2]. Peppa, Elsa and Shrek have all been caught up.

The discussion around editorial content has led to the consideration of editorial standards online. This is a question that first made headlines following YouTube maker Logan Paul's video[3] that featured victims of suicide in Japan. It's created lots of discussion, but two notable commentaries

1 http://uk.businessinsider.com/ap-germany-bans-childrens-smart-watches-with-listening-app-2017-11

2 https://www.polygon.com/2017/12/8/16737556/youtube-kids-video-inappropriate-superhero-disney

3 https://www.huffingtonpost.co.uk/entry/logan-paul-youtube-blasted-video_us_5a4b3372e4b06d1621ba4eb3

came from James Bridle on Medium[4] and CBBC's Ed Petrie, initially a *Guardian* interview[5] and now developed by Ed in this Yearbook. Both are worth a read.

Then, in December last year, after weeks of suggesting that the content a child saw was the responsibility of parents, You Tube bowed to pressure and announced that it would be recruiting thousands of human moderators[6].

While the news focuses on algorithms, there are underlying issues that have to be addressed by government and society. The controversies around the use of Facebook data in the US election and the EU referendum are alarming, but it goes much further than that: one report, for instance, even accuses the platform of using the emotional state of teenagers to target advertising[7].

At the core is a debate about the value and ownership of data. In March, we learnt that Facebook shared data on millions of users. We've become used to an internet and vital everyday websites that are free at the point of use, but to pay for that access users are trading their personal data which, as Facebook's revenue highlights, has value far beyond the costs of the service provided. If

adults struggle with that concept, how can children make informed decisions on the data they share?

The platforms would argue that they have done nothing wrong: users agree to terms and conditions, which allow the platforms to exploit the data – and besides, they say, children shouldn't be on those platforms anyway. In many ways, they're right. However, the argument that children are not using social platforms weakens every day[8]. And let's face it – if Facebook can serve me an ad based on its analysis of my interests, it can probably work out if a user is under 13.

The question for us, for kids as consumers, and equally importantly for the companies themselves in terms of relationship-building with their customers, is whether users understand the implications of sharing data and can make an informed decision. In addition, as the platforms evolve, do users continue to understand how that data can be used? Obviously these issues are particularly pertinent to children's use of the internet.

One of the outcomes of these months of controversy is that internet safety has risen steadily to the top of the government's agenda. In spring 2017 the Digital Economy Act passed into law, creating new rules including age verification to ensure users of legal porn sites are over 18. That was followed by a Lords' report and subsequent government Green Paper on Child Internet

----

4 https://medium.com/@jamesbridle/something-is-wrong-on-the-internet-c39c471271d2

5 https://www.theguardian.com/tv-and-radio/2018/jan/09/how-childrens-tv-went-from-blue-peter-to-youtube-wild-west?CMP=Share_iOSApp_Other

6 https://mashable.com/2017/12/04/youtube-ceo-human-moderators-violent-kids-videos/#mZVp4VxKMsqD

7 https://www.theguardian.com/technology/2017/may/01/facebook-advertising-data-insecure-teens

----

8 http://www.bbc.com/news/technology-42153694

Safety[9]. Then a few weeks ago in May, the government published a response to the consultation on the Green Paper[10], promising new regulation.

For many in the digital industry, that's an alarming prospect. However, with the internet so pervasive and with so many issues surfacing, it's hard to argue that continued self-regulation is sustainable. Reassuringly, the Secretary of State at DCMS, Matt Hancock, has clarified that he's expecting the internet to be brought into line with existing legislation for other platforms rather than a raft of bespoke laws. This is a position that's been advocated by the CMF: we think classifying online platforms as publishers rather than merely distributors – especially as many are directly commissioning content – would significantly change their legal responsibility and could be a useful first step.

Unfortunately, none of the current controversies are new. Many of the issues being reported now have been predicted and championed by the CMF for months (even years) in our various submissions[11] to parliamentary consultations and public statements. These submissions are based on insight, research and understanding of the children's audience – something that is still lacking at the social media platforms. Now, it would appear that children have been the "canaries in the coalmine" when it comes to internet safety, integrity and responsible relationships between providers and their users. And as the social media platforms start to think seriously about their bottom-line and their shareholders – in light of keeping their customers happy – the time could be ripe for a greater acceptance of their role in being part of the village that brings up our kids…

We hope this might also mean that children's needs are given greater weight in the policy-making process. Certainly they are on the government and press agendas, and parents have at last been empowered to speak out about what concerns them.

The role of the CMF will be to seek not knee-jerk reactions, but reasoned and reasonable responses that are deliverable in the real world, reflecting the pervasive nature of social media for good and ill and the need for all parties to work together to make sure kids get the very best of the internet, with protection from the worst. ○

9 https://assets.publishing.service.gov.uk/government/uploads/system/uploads/attachment_data/file/650949/Internet_Safety_Strategy_green_paper.pdf

10 https://assets.publishing.service.gov.uk/government/uploads/system/uploads/attachment_data/file/708873/Government_Response_to_the_Internet_Safety_Strategy_Green_Paper_-_Final.pdf

11 http://www.thechildrensmediafoundation.org/action

VR + KIDS: A UK RESEARCH ROADSHOW FOR THE CHILDREN'S MEDIA FOUNDATION

ALISON NORRINGTON

—

"Any sufficiently advanced technology is indistinguishable from magic."
Arthur C. Clarke

2017 saw virtual reality debut at the Children's Media Conference (CMC) across four tracks; from a workshop where participants prototyped a scene from a well-known nursery rhyme, to more nitty-gritty topics ranging from **Ethics & Policy, Distribution & Monetisation** to **The Creative Challenge.**

A year later, VR+Kids is still Marmite. It continues to raise eyebrows along with very valid concerns and, for the record, despite consulting and mentoring story and VR development, I remain an excited sceptic. But I also feel a strong sense of responsibility as a story-teller and experience designer. As technology advances at lightning speed, it's evident that VR is here to stay, and as story-tellers and content creators we can't be ostriches. So, when the Children's Media Foundation asked me to continue the conversations around virtual and mixed reality that we started at CMC 2017 and to lead further research on VR+Kids, I jumped at the chance, with a focus on three core research areas:

1. **Appropriateness:** the evolution of best practices for the design of VR content for children that compares duration, immersion, story-centred, learning-based experiences.
2. **Cognitive and Sensory Health & Safety:** scientific progress and studies into overloading children through VR experiences along with best practices.
3. **Eye health and Balance:** scientific progress and research into ongoing

visual and balance implications and best practices.

Faced with the prospect of reading endless opinion pieces, I decided to take this to the people studying and making this content and so the Children's Media Foundation VR+Kids Research Roadshow was born.

With a UK round trip from Leeds to Bristol, here's how it works. Four cities over a year – each event invitation-only and focusing on four different design concerns around kids and VR. From each chapter, elements of a design brief are created by the group – in which there are *no attendees, only participants* – culminating in a final live rapid-prototyping session with Digital Directions students at the Royal College of Art (RCA) in December 2018.

Our kick-off event, **Crossing Physical & Virtual Worlds in Kids VR**, was co-produced with Dr Dylan Yamada-Rice and hosted by Dubit in Leeds on Tuesday 27 March 2018. With a format of five 15-minute conversation-starters, we covered topics from **Design Standards for Place-Based Immersive Experiences** to **Producer Perspectives: Storytelling Across Domains**. With a mix of academics and practitioners around the table, we also debated best practices on **Children Creating in Physical & Virtual Spaces**. CMC 2017 VR speaker Professor Mark Mon-Williams shared some exciting and potentially game-changing research on **Designing for Good Eye Health** and RCA professors joined us to speak about **Digital Directions**.

Dr Eleanor Dare concluded the Leeds round table by stating:

"It's important, when researching best practices in VR, that we define the differences between what's happening commercially, what's happening artistically and what's happening in academic research."

NARRATIVE DESIGN FOR VR + KIDS
Tuesday 26th June 2018, 15:00 - 18:00pm
produced by storycentralLABS for **The Children's Media Foundation**, hosted by Immersive Storytelling Studio, **National Theatre**, London

The 2nd in a series of VR • Kids UK Roadshow for The Children's Media Foundation

The London chapter took place on Tuesday 26 June, hosted at the National Theatre's Immersive Storytelling Studio, and looked at **Narrative Design for VR+ Kids**, focusing on four topics:
- **Story Arcs & Roller Coasters – For Kids**
- **Narrative Design as Structure**
- **Replayable Stories vs Episodic Bridges**
- **Theatre & VR: Immersion & 4th Walls**

The research so far suggests huge parallels with the semantics of comic book and cartoon structure, and suggests that VR experiences could be/should be developed

CROSSING PHYSICAL & VIRTUAL WORLDS IN KIDS VR
Tuesday 27th March 2018, 15:00 - 17:00pm
produced by storycentralLABS for The Children's Media Foundation, hosted by Dubit, Leeds

The 1st in a series of
VR • Kids UK Roadshow for
The Children's Media Foundation

to dovetail with medical advancements such as lazy eye treatment or rehabilitation for children through story-telling and experiences. A core point has already been raised – the fact that kids predominantly use their bodies differently from adults.

The Manchester and Bristol chapters are scheduled for September and November. The Manchester chapter will take a

CONJURING MAGICAL EXPERIENCES FOR KIDS VR
Tuesday 25th September 2018, 3:00- 6.00pm
produced by storycentralLABS for The Children's Media Foundation

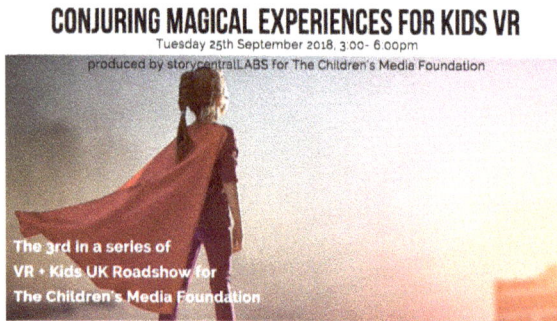

The 3rd in a series of
VR + Kids UK Roadshow for
The Children's Media Foundation

close look, encourage debate and share knowledge exchange on:

- Ontological Design & Spatial Awareness
- Experience Design in VR – What To Do?
- VR+ Kids: A Broadcaster's POV
- The Health & Safety Issue of Controlled Experiences

The Bristol chapter promises to raise discussion on further best practices around:

- Eliciting Emotions Through Story
- Managing Expectations & Emotional Fallout

MAKING KIDS FEEL : EMOTIONAL DESIGN FOR KIDS IN VR
Tuesday 27th November 2018, 15:00- 18:00pm
produced by storycentralLABS for The Children's Media Foundation

The 4th in a series of
VR + Kids UK Roadshow for
The Children's Media Foundation

"Consider what are the triggers that make the Virtual Reality experience better than reality? If there is nothing–then what is the point?"
Dr Dylan Yamada-Rice

As with all five installments of this Research Roadshow, we will continue to compile an infographic on the key points of best practices so far. These points will form the basis of a brief, which will be built upon over the four events, culminating in the prototyping session led by Alison Norrington and Dr Dylan Yamada-Rice at RCA in December 2018.

Write-ups for each topic and round table can be found at http://bit.ly/CMFVRKidsDubitPartOne.

CONNECTED GRANDPARENTS: ARE SMART TOYS THE FUTURE FOR INTERGENERATIONAL PLAY?

ANNA TAYLOR AND FIONA PEARCE

Playtime as we know it has changed rapidly in the last few years, with technology now an established part of play and leisure activity for children.

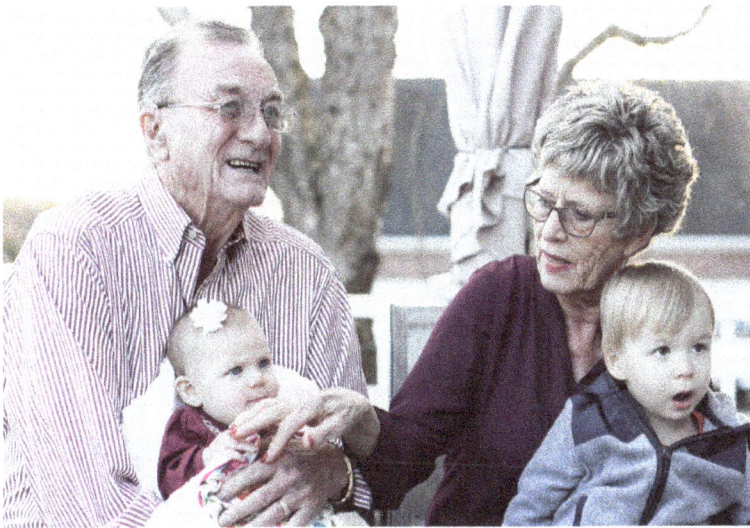

In the US, children under eight years old typically spend around 25 minutes a day gaming on electronic devices (Common Sense Media, 2017, page 13), while 66% of 8–12-year-olds (Common Sense Media, 2015, page 24) in the US use technology for gaming, with mobile games being the most popular. Grandparents often enjoy sharing the toys and games they remember from their own youth with their grandchildren, and while digital gaming shouldn't replace this, research suggests that introducing technology to intergenerational playtime may help strengthen that valuable grandparent–grandchild relationship.

Typically, when a grandchild and a grandparent play together, the grandparent is the more experienced player and so takes on the role of the mentor. But with digital gaming the roles are reversed, giving the grandchild the opportunity to take the lead (Aarsand, 2007). In addition, grandparents gain the support of a more experienced digital user while also enjoying the social side of gaming (Osmanovic & Pecchioni, 2016).

The majority of the research in the area of intergenerational digital gaming has largely concentrated on the use of games consoles (Aarsand et al., 2007; Chua et al. 2013; Vanden Abeele & Deschutter, 2010; Xu et al.,

2016). However, in recent years the popularity of games consoles has fallen rapidly (from 91% in 2011 to 86% in 2017; Ofcom, 2017) while there has been a sharp increase in the number of children using tablet devices (from 7% in 2011 to 86% in 2017). Meanwhile, smart toys (some of which connect to a tablet device) represent an increasingly popular area within the toy market, with worldwide sales predicted to grow from $4.9bn in 2017 to $15.5bn by 2022 (Juniper Research, 2017).

The focus of our research (currently in progress) is to investigate the attitudes of grandparents towards digital play, with a particular focus on smart toys. Unlike many mobile games and consoles where players must learn to use controls, smart toys use tangible objects that can often be used to interact with a screen. We are interested to find out whether this makes the technology more accessible to the older generation, as controls can present a barrier to play (e.g. Aarsand et al., 2007, excerpt 2, page 244), without the child losing their new role as a digital teacher.

The data so far suggests that attitudes towards digital gaming may be very divided, but we do seem to be seeing a group of grandparents emerge who enjoy using technology and are somewhat confident in their digital literacy. Although overall interest in trying new technology (e.g. smart home products) has been very mixed, responses suggest that grandparents may be a little more open to using it as a way to play with their grandchildren. The next stage of our research will explore the reasoning behind these attitudes, with the aim of understanding why a grandparent may or may not choose to engage in digital gaming with their grandchild.

Being mindful that this is very early data, the pattern so far suggests that grandparents are willing to use technology to play games with their grandchild, despite a certain level of apprehension. This indicates that both digital gaming and smart toys may indeed have a place in intergenerational play.

References

Aarsand, P. A., Linkpings, U., Filosofiska, F., Institutionen fr, t., & Tema, B. (2007). *Computer and Video Games in Family Life: The digital divide as a resource in intergenerational interactions.* Childhood, 14(2), 235-256. doi:10.1177/0907568207078330

Chua, P.H., Jung, Y., Lwin, M. O., & Theng, Y.-L. (2013). Let's play together: Effects of video-game play on intergenerational perceptions among youth and elderly participants. *Computers in Human Behavior*, 29(6), 2303-2311. doi:10.1016/j.chb.2013.04.037

Common Sense Media (2015). The common sense census: media use by tweens and teens. Retrieved from: "http://cdn.cnn.com/cnn/2017/images/11/07/commonsensecensus.mediausebytweensandteens.2015.final.pdf"

Common Sense Media (2017). The common sense census: media use by kids age zero to eight. Retrieved from: "http://cdn.cnn.com/cnn/2017/images/11/07/csm_zerotoeight_full.report.final.2017.pdf"

Juniper Research (2017). Juniper Research: Smart Toy Sales to Grow Threefold to Exceed $15.5 Billion by 2022. Retrieved from "https://www.juniperresearch.com/press/press-releases/smart-toy-sales-to-grow-threefold"

Ofcom (2017). Devices available to children in the home in the United Kingdom (UK) from 2011 to 2017. Retrieved from "https://www.ofcom.org.uk/__data/assets/pdf_file/0020/108182/children-parents-media-use-attitudes-2017.pdf"

Osmanovic, S., & Pecchioni, L. (2016). Beyond Entertainment: Motivations and Outcomes of Video Game Playing by Older Adults and Their Younger Family Members. *Games and Culture*, 11(1-2), 130-149. doi:10.1177/1555412015602819

Vanden Abeele, V., & De Schutter, B. (2010). Designing intergenerational play via enactive interaction, competition and acceleration. *Personal and Ubiquitous Computing*, 14(5), 425-433. doi:10.1007/s00779-009-0262-3

Xu, X., Li, J., Pham, T.P., Salmon, C.T., & Theng, Y.-L. (2016). Improving Psychosocial Well-Being of Older Adults Through Exergaming: The Moderation Effects of Intergenerational Communication and Age Cohorts. *Games Health* J, 5, 389–397.

UNDERSTANDING EMERGING CULTURE: CREATING MEANINGFUL FUTURES FOR CHILDREN'S BRANDS

CATO HUNT AND COLETTE SENSIER

—

Children's media and brands are part of an ever-changing cultural context; they have the power to both reflect and shape culture. Broad cultural shifts (demonstrated in everything from pop music to food packaging) will influence children's and parents' behaviours and self-perceptions – and their feelings towards brands. A brand can keep doing exactly the same thing, and have its meaning changed as culture moves on (just ask *The Simpsons*' Apu Nahasapeemapetilon…).

But brands can continuously respond to new cultural shifts through using semiotics, helping them become cultural leaders through shaping future meanings. By decoding how meaning is communicated through the signs and symbols we see every day, we can reveal the subconscious drivers that power human decision-making.

Every detail matters. A colour, typeface, texture, sound, setting, scent, gesture. These all add up to a meaning, influenced by cultural myths and beliefs. That's why Space Doctors' mantra is: Everything Communicates. Brands are bundles of meanings and associations, coming from the sum total of their products, communications, activities and behaviours. Semiotics helps communicators to read these bundles in the light of Right Now; and work out what might need changing as culture shifts.

For instance, we recently explored

the communication and stories around children's dolls, from Disney princesses to Barbie and American Girl. We were looking to identify the cultural conditioning acting on girls as they develop a sense of self-awareness and of limitations. Which stories hold girls back from realising their potential, and to what extent were these brands perpetuating them?

Nowadays, no toy brand wants to convey the message that girls can only like shopping, housework or getting their hair done. But in semiotics, real meaning is often conveyed in how you're saying or doing something, rather than what you're saying or doing.

Across the whole doll category, subtle cues were driving home the message that girls should stay at home, pay attention, and care for others before themselves.

We found, for example, that while brands thought they were presenting a huge range of activity options for girls, the fact that there were discrete options – do you want to be an explorer with special goggles, or a vet with an operating table? – made girls' choices feel limited. Boys' toys tended to give them key objects which could be used in many different types of pretend games, stimulating their imaginations and ability to fantasise, rather than giving them the pre-defined narratives and worlds embedded in girls' toys.

Marketers and brand builders always aim to shape their brand's meaning by telling the most compelling stories, embedding them more strongly in consumers' minds over time. But frequently, there is a chasm between the original intention and how the end experience is received. Were the notions of "limited" choice for girls deliberate? If they weren't, then something got lost in translation. And if they were, then this is completely out of touch in a culture where influential figures from male make-up models to *Black Panther*'s Dora Milaje female warriors prove that anyone can be anything. Either way, this is where semiotics can be a powerful tool, helping us to understand how to better connect with culture, and "tune up" what it is we want to say.

Semiotics enables us to "decode" brands and their competitive set – unique intelligence for any brand. What makes you strong and distinctive in people's minds? What is diluting your intention or strategy? What can you build on to make your brand better connect with your audience?

To do this, we look for patterns of meaning in culture, and break these down into themes we call codes. A code represents the shared dimension of thinking that shapes beliefs, attitudes, and behaviour, identifying the key assumptions that underpin a cultural idea. For example, there will be different codes of ideas prevalent in children's brands and media, like "family", "play" and "adventure". Semiotics enables us to understand the different ways in which these ideas can come to life with greater nuance. It not only helps deliver greater clarity in what we want to say, but also functions as creative inspiration, showing us different versions of the ideas we could explore further.

Some codes reflect current culture, which we call *dominant*, but we're most interested in the *emergent*, the signs of cultural change that mean our stories and brands can actively shape culture. It's important that children's media reflects the newest meanings around their products and opinions about society in order to prepare children for the future. Being at the cutting edge of these ideas means understanding which new myths are arising in culture – not just within your own category – and which of them you're already connecting to, or which you *could* connect to.

Using semiotics can positively shape culture with intent, helping children's media brands to create more meaningful futures for their audiences. Semiotics can deliver the nudge which in turn makes large-scale behavioural change possible – and can show how to deliver that nudge in a way which makes sense for your brand.

Ultimately, a semiotic approach is a new way of seeing. Marketers understand their brand through new eyes, revealing new opportunities to drive a brand's cultural relevance and impact. Creatives benefit because the brief becomes crystal clear, opening up unseen creative possibility. By identifying specific equities and their roles in signs and myths, a piece of media or communication can become a potent embodiment of intended meaning, amplifying brand impact and memorability as well as sounding a truly resonant voice for cultural change. ◯

BEAUTY AND THE BEAST

LESLEY SALEM AND CHLOE BARTLEM

—

Razor Kids is a specialist kids, youth and family unit at Razor Research, a full-service market research agency based in London.

Each school term, we use a fresh set of Roving Reporters to explore a topic of interest. This spring, inspired by International Women's Day, we launched The Beauty Project, examining the perceptions of tween and teen girls around beauty and self-image, particularly with regard to active social media use. There's been a lot of negative press on this subject recently and so we wanted to explore the truth of such claims – to identify beauty tensions, positive role models and influencers, as well as relevant, compelling ways young females want media and brands to portray beauty. Our study findings are based on a qualitative approach. In March, we spoke in depth to 26 girls aged 8–14 across the UK on a range of questions. We are looking forward to sharing our videos and findings at the 2018 Children's Media Conference. As we plan our next wave of research, we welcome attendees to send in their specific requests of exploration to: lesley@razorresearch.co.uk and chloebartlem@razorresearch.co.uk

If you listen to girls talk about what it's like growing up in 2018, on the surface it sounds positive. They have greater aspirations and opportunities for their careers, along with an array of positive female role models to emulate. Many cite their mums as aspirational figures. The rhetoric at schools educates girls that there are wider definitions around identity and greater acceptance around diversity. Principles we take for granted like gender, routes to success and identity are being reappraised with a critical eye. They have multiple opportunities to express their individuality, values and beliefs. Sexuality doesn't have to be set in stone. However, media content and advertising imagery still presents the world with a very narrowly defined view of what is regarded as socially acceptable and idealised norms.

Transitioning into a teenager always comes with angst, self-doubt, and a need for peer acceptance but this has been exacerbated for teens who are active on social media as they share and live their lives under public scrutiny, accelerated into adult worlds. A short cut to feeling popular is wearing make-up. Girls as young as nine years old are regularly buying cosmetics (often at adult price tags), viewing YouTube tutorials on beauty hacks and following beauty influencers and vloggers. As more girls their age wear make-up, this becomes the norm and those who are not allowed to, or simply don't want to, are left feeling excluded. Even those not wearing make-up feel compelled to post selfies that will increase their "likes", delete posts if they've not been liked, take photos to keep their "streaks" up and curate imagery to show the world all the "amazing" and "epic" things they are up to.

Given their tender age, it isn't surprising that they don't all have the emotional resilience to cope with being judged so openly and harshly. Our study found that regardless of location, family set-up or age, as soon as girls become active on social media, they tend to experience feelings of insecurity about the way they look. We've coined this "The Beauty Gap".

In a visual culture of enhancement through filters, photoshopping and editing, the benchmarks of beauty and self-image have been raised to new heights. It's much harder to work out who is a professional model, who is a celebrity and who is a peer. This creates a new norm of unattainable beauty for many. Whilst some girls are able to improve the way their present themselves digitally, they talk about feeling ugly in real life.

"Because people use filters and photoshop on their pictures, it makes me think my own image isn't good enough."
14-year-old, Year 10, London

"I do feel like I pressure myself. If I see someone who looks really pretty on all of their photos, then I look at my photos and I think, why do I not look like that. Why am I not as pretty as her?"
11-year-old, Year 6, Crewe

Whilst tweens and teens often follow the crowd, it's also interesting to note grumblings and frustrations, particularly from girls aged 12–14 who feel this pressure more acutely than the younger girls in our sample. They strongly criticise the beauty industry and media for not doing enough to represent real and diverse beauty in its imagery and messaging. They lament that social media relentlessly feeds them images that all look the same. We sense that this is an early indicator of a more activist movement that will be displayed by this generation as they age.

The icons and influencers these girls look up to and respect are quite different from those admired by their older peers. They go for people with strong inner qualities. Those that use fame or misfortune to make a difference. People that display positivity and a can-do attitude. Those that support causes they affiliate with and have a social conscience. Others that demonstrate bravery and boldness in being themselves and pushing boundaries (i.e. Nikki Lilly). Embracing diversity is also reflected in the rise in popularity of transgender vloggers, such as James Charles and Patrick Starr.

The time is ripe to celebrate real beauty that emphasises what's inside and allows girls to be proud of their quirks and uniquely defining beauty marks. Girls growing up today truly believe that the world is a better place with diversity and as the undercurrent of discontent grows, media brands need to be seen as offering content; messaging and selecting talent that's more representative, if they are to establish an affinity with our next generation of women.

○

CHILDREN'S SCREEN CONTENT IN AN ERA OF FORCED MIGRATION: MISSING VOICES, DIVERSITY, AND QUESTIONS OF ETHICS[1]

NAOMI SAKR, CHRISTINE SINGER AND JEANETTE STEEMERS

—

Displaced children have comprised a small but growing segment of diverse child audiences across Europe[2] since 2014 and 2015, when thousands of Arabic-speaking families, mostly from Syria and Iraq, were forced to flee their homelands for Europe because of war. Although the crisis has been covered extensively in the news, the personal accounts of children who have experienced forced migration remain largely absent[3]– except when it is too late, as demonstrated by photos of the body of three-year-old Aylan Kurdi, washed ashore on a Turkish beach in 2015. Fair representation of displaced children in children's drama and factual content can accomplish two things. Firstly, by seeing children like themselves onscreen, the new arrivals can start to feel a sense of belonging at home in a new country. But secondly, children's content can help European-born children to better understand what it's like to have to start a new life and find new friends.

1   This work was supported by the Arts and Humanities Research Council [Grant: AH/ R001421/1] as *Collaborative Development of Children's Screen Content in an Era of Forced Migration Flows: Facilitating Arab-European Dialogue*.

2   According to statistics from the UN Refugee Agency, UNHCR, the UK gave asylum or other protection to 28,000 children in the seven years to February 2017.

3   Gillespie, Marie, Lawrence Ampofo, Margaret Cheesman et al. *Mapping Syrian Refugee Media Journeys: Smartphones and Social Media Networks*, The Open University and France Médias Monde, May 2016.

Our project, funded by the UK's Arts and Humanities Research Council (AHRC) and informed by findings from our earlier AHRC-funded research into children's media industries and child audiences in the Arab world, focuses on screen content made in Europe, featuring children from migrant backgrounds, including those who have experienced forced migration. Through a series of workshops in Manchester, Copenhagen and Munich, we have got European and Arab producers, rights advocates, and broadcasters to talk together about what works best if we want to engage all types of children with European content that deals with migration, but also gives more broadly diverse representations that reflect the ethnic, class and gender make-up of our societies[4]. In a rapidly changing children's market, where we are frequently told that children no longer watch "TV" and only want entertainment, how can we find ways of funding and distributing content that has something engaging and entertaining to say about being an informed citizen?

4   For the individual workshop reports see: https:// euroarabchildrensmedia.org/ reports/

Challenges of funding and distribution

Across Europe there are very few children's dramas, animation series or documentaries that represent migrant children, ethnically diverse communities or even children who simply live in countries outside Europe. Those that do exist have been commissioned largely by public service broadcasters (PSBs). Notable recent examples include CBBC's commission *New Boys in Town* (Drummer TV, 2017) focusing on 12-year-old Adel, a Syrian refugee recently settled in Bristol as part of the *My Life* strand. Another is CBeebies' pre-school soap, *Apple Tree House* (Five Apples, 2017), with its ethnically diverse cast and some storylines that touch on migration. Other key European players include public service commissioners in Scandinavia (Danmarks Radio/DR, NRK), the Netherlands (KRO-NCRV) and Germany (ZDF, WDR). Yet even they are struggling to justify commissions, in a world where they are not just competing with the US transnationals like Disney and Nickelodeon, but also with YouTube. Reflecting on home-grown children's drama and documentaries, including those

that cover migration issues, a Scandinavian broadcast executive told us, "the issue is that we don't know how to use them". In addition to TV, Scandinavian and Dutch broadcasters distribute them through schools, film festivals and their own online channels, often working closely with national film institutes. One exception was *Hassan and Ramadan*, which DR released as a web series of 17 episodes on YouTube in 2017. This racked up an impressive 100,000 views per episode in a small country, but broadcasters don't know why, underlining how little we know about what children actually value, just as video-on-demand (Netflix, YouTube) and social media (Facebook) players exploit their proprietary access to more granular algorithmic data.

A well-planned, multi-media distribution strategy is of course the holy grail, but funding needs to be in place first, and this is getting more difficult to access across Europe. As one Danish producer remarked, "I never met a funder who said: 'I will not promote diversity'. But the problem is the distribution. The problem is that they [commissioners] are very scared of throwing their money towards something that is not being used, which is understandable." Without solving the distribution issue, the alternative for European content focused on diversity is "to live a very, very lonely life on some internet platforms".

Ethical questions

Beyond the perennial issues of funding and distribution, which impact on all domestically produced children's content in Europe, are issues of ethics: how do you represent displaced children in animation, drama and factual content without making them look, even unintentionally, like victims? This needs to be looked at from two angles. On the one hand there is content aimed at European-born children to help them understand why forced migration is taking place. Longer term, there is also content that shows newly arrived children in their new countries, and how they are adjusting to new friends and situations, and balancing this with their family and cultural identities.

Factual reports in children's news (e.g. the BBC's *Newsround* or ZDF's *Logo*), and European children's documentaries, which focus on children's flight from places like Syria, or their lives in refugee camps, can be problematic. Fundamentally these are about informing European-born audiences about what is happening. The challenge is in achieving a balance between getting too close to refugee children and standing too far back. Examples highlighted by both Arab and European practitioners included filming children in refugee camps without asking their consent ("too close"), and filming with concealed faces and limited back stories, making it difficult for European-born children to identify with the children being filmed. Against the backdrop of rising anti-immigration sentiments across Europe, it's important for film-makers to get it right, so that children can empathise, identify similarities and connections.

"Show the diversity, don't name it"

Once you move away from showing children's immediate experiences of flight, how do film-makers move on to show how children are getting on with their lives in new surroundings, without labelling children as "refugees", "migrants", and "Arabs" – or crediting them

with attitudes in ways that risk tapping into stereotypes, that may marginalise them as fundamentally different from children in the host community? One hurdle lies in the poor representation of people with minority backgrounds among directors, writers, producers, and financiers in the business. These imbalances mean that diverse stories that cut across ethnicity, class and gender rarely rise to the top of the pile when it comes to new projects.

Another issue is how to represent diversity without becoming heavy-handed. Most writers and producers would say they tackle this by weaving issues of diversity into appealing stories and characters, without diversity being the key object of the narrative. For example, CBeebies' *Apple Tree House* is about a group of young friends from diverse backgrounds who live on a UK council estate, and overcome childhood dilemmas, without ethnicity being an issue at all. Similarly, the Dutch film *Heijplaters* (*Harbourboyz*, 2018) concentrates on the friendships and similarities among a group of ethnically diverse boys (Turkish, Syrian, Chinese, Surinamese, and Dutch) who live in the harbour district of Rotterdam. As the directors suggest: "You can show the diversity, don't name it", and this is done by focusing on the things they do together such as swimming in the harbour, rapping and playing football rather than making their background the major focus of the story.

At other times, ethnic origin is an intrinsic part of the story. For example, the German drama series *Dschermeni* (ZDF, 2017) focuses on the adventures of a young group of friends including German-born children and migrant children living in an asylum centre. The series doesn't shy away from the fact that one of the friends has to return to her country of origin, during the course of the series, but this is just one storyline among many others that are not migration focused. By contrast, *Children's Mayor* (KRO-NCRV, 2017) from the Netherlands has at its core the real-life story of Yassine, a Moroccan-Dutch boy, who becomes children's mayor of Gouda for a year, and is not afraid of putting his role model, the Moroccan-born mayor of Rotterdam, Ahmed Aboutaleb, on the spot. The point in this case is to present a story about a boy with a dream of becoming a politician, and children who "can be what they want to be".

Above all some of the key lessons to be learned from encounters between Arab and European media professionals are that we should:

- Make more local content in which children **see others like themselves** on screen. Children newly arrived in Europe benefit from seeing others like them adapting to their new environment. **Focus on strong characters** rather than victims. And **address the gender gap** – more films are needed that address girls' experience of migration.
- **Show diversity, don't name it**. Avoid making difference the focus of the story, and try to establish similarities and connections between newly arrived children and children of the host community.
- **Work with children, not for them**. As well as casting them in professional productions, this also means consulting them and getting them involved in production processes.
- **Find similarities** between children who are new to a country and those already there. Children often feel empowered if they see themselves sharing something they know with their new friends, whether it's their music, drawing or something "as simple as kicking a ball and scoring a goal, or helping to solve some kind of problem".
- **Be mindful of ethics**. There are ethical implications in publicly touching on the painful past of young refugees.

Project reports for this research can be accessed and downloaded here:

https://euroarabchildrensmedia.org/reports/

A symposium on "INVISIBLE CHILDREN: PUBLIC SERVICE MEDIA, DIVERSITY AND FORCED MIGRATION" will be held at the Anatomy Museum, King's College London on 14 September 2018. To find out more, visit: https://euroarabchildrensmedia.org/london-symposium/ or email: Christine.Singer@kcl.ac.uk

IN AN EVER-CONNECTED WORLD, CHILDREN ARE BECOMING INCREASINGLY DISCONNECTED

NICK RICHARDSON

———

As we know, children are growing up in a constantly changing world, with technology playing an ever-increasing role in their lives.

We're seeing shifts in the ways kids use and engage with technology, from how "generation type" became "generation swipe", to the evolution of "generation speak". Our data shows that 28% of children under the age of 10 can already control their tablet with their voice, and 1 in 10 of all kids now use Alexa in their home.

Focusing specifically on tablets, our data shows a continued increase in popularity. 75% of 4–6-year-olds now own one, compared to 65% last year.

There has been a reduction in access and ownership when it comes to other devices. In fact, TV and consoles – both of which were once the nucleus of the children's ecosystem – have seen a significant drop, falling by 9% and 8% amongst 4–6-year-olds respectively.

It's not just device ownership and access which is changing, but also the way children are consuming content. For instance, binge-watching of multiple episodes in one sitting continues to reduce. The number of children aged 4–18 who watch multiple episodes of a TV show in one sitting has decreased from 98% in late 2016 to 80% in 2018.

The sheer amount of content that children have access to continues to grow, with over 100 Freeview channels, several hundred Sky channels, and a seemingly limitless stream of content from Netflix, Amazon and YouTube.

Device Access (Q1 2018, % Change from Q3 2017)					
	Console	**Laptop**	**Mobile**	**Tablet**	**TV**
4 to 6	44% (-9%)	35% (-3%)	41% (-4%)	86% (5%)	72% (-8%)
7 to 9	65% (-9%)	54% (-12%)	51% (-2%)	80% (-3%)	77% (-6%)
10 to 12	75% (1%)	71% (-3%)	74% (-2%)	80% (2%)	83% (1%)
13 to 15	74% (5%)	76% (-3%)	89% (1%)	72% (0%)	87% (2%)
16 to 18	66% (6%)	83% (1%)	94% (-2%)	65% (-4%)	82% (-6%)

Despite children having more choice than ever before, we're seeing evidence that kids' attention is becoming more focused, as they concentrate solely on content they love. This means brands are increasingly stretching their ecosystem, with no better example of this in our data than LEGO.

LEGO's core market of toys and bricks dominate their competition, and as a result are favourites of children under 13. Onscreen, the LEGO Batman and Ninjago movies have scored as the top films for boys over the last 12 months. Likewise, the main characters of each films have also reached the top ten with children, as do the LEGO video games on console, which are currently the third favourite of under-13s.

LEGO is also increasingly reaching a slightly older demographic, combining technology and LEGO building with its latest Powered Up range, enabling children to build and code remote-controlled vehicles, merging the digital and physical play worlds further.

When it comes to LEGO magazines, *LEGO Club*, *Friends*, *Ninjago* and *Star Wars* titles are currently extremely popular with pre-teens. Unprompted, children state visiting LEGOLAND as one of the most popular answers when asked to describe their dream day.

Essentially, children who are LEGO fans are spending increased time within the LEGO ecosystem.

As children immerse themselves in this way, their own individual microsystems become increasingly niche and disconnected from their wider ecosystem.

We also see this happening in sport, especially with the Manchester United brand, which is currently one of the fastest growing YouTube channels. Likewise, Minecraft, the favourite video game of the under-13s, has successfully moved into books, and currently occupies two of the top ten favourite titles with tweens.

Implications and Opportunities

Successful brands are changing their approach and strategy by building multi-dimensional ecosystems, with larger footprints and an audience-centric approach as they fight for the attention of children.

Traditionally, brands would remain

in their own specific territories, with any expansion predominantly down to brand licensing strategy. However, this is no longer the case. Brands are now developing an immersive ecosystem which provides a never-ending supply of content, engaging children across multiple platforms, products and experiences.

Rather than relying on straightforward licensing agreements, deeper partnerships and collaborations to create enriching content are key. It also shows the importance of brand-led over-the-top (OTT) media platforms, which serve content directly to the consumer to provide more tailored and relevant content directly to their audience.

So, we know that children's ecosystems are becoming more fragmented and complex as technology plays an increasingly large role in their lives. However, despite having a never-ending stream of content, our data shows that children's focus and attention is becoming more concentrated on specific areas.

We look forward to embarking on the next part of our international expansion, with Kids Insights USA launching in September. This will see us surveying more than 800 different children every single week and adding 300,000 data points into our online portal, in real time. ◯

To discover more and download a free report, visit http://www.kidsinsights.co.uk/yearbook

All data taken from Kids Insights UK Q1 2018 Reports

www.kidsinsights.co.uk

LGBT STORYLINES IN CHILDREN'S TV

DAVID LEVINE

The Lodge

Introduction

What is it like to grow up with TV shows that don't reflect your own core beliefs and values, your own life experiences and personal appearance? For those of us who grew up in the '70s or early '80s, that was the reality for many when it came to children's television. We had great cartoons, but the creation of truly reflective kid-focused episodic programming didn't hit until the mid-'90s, when shows quickly began to include, at the very least, the ethnic and cultural diversity of their audiences. As an industry, we have come even further in 2018, but there is still work to be done.

In the past few years, we have seen a further evolution in this trend, incorporating LGBT characters and themes into kids' programming. It is a start but how can we ensure that we continue to reflect modern society in children's content? Where and how can the industry continue to make a difference?

Looking Back

Growing up as a kid in the '70's and '80s in the US, the entertainment choices were much more limited in scope than today – no kids' cable channels, no SVOD services, no online video – mostly a staple of cartoons on linear terrestrial television during the after school hours and weekend mornings, with a diet of general entertainment action/adventure shows. The idea of seeing "real kids" in media was exceptionally rare. The live action content of the late '80s was limited to variety shows and the occasional drama – the original *Degrassi Junior High* could be found on the smaller public television stations, and when it premiered it showed relevant stories that were among the first of its kind. Notably the show had an episode with an LGBT storyline, which was not aired in the UK at the time.

Growing up as a Marvel comic book-collecting Jewish kid on Long Island, the representations of similar characters in popular media were virtually non-existent. The day I opened up *X-Men 239* with the first appearance of the Jewish star-wearing Kitty Pride, my heart swelled. Finally, there was a visibly Jewish character in my beloved Marvel comics. As a teenager trying to figure out my sexuality in the mid '80s, there were no role models, and without the internet, there were few ways to discreetly obtain any information about what it meant to be gay – parts of my education came from stand-up comedy shows. It wouldn't be until years later, with the groundbreaking Pedro in *The Real World* followed by the UK's *Queer as Folk*, that I began to see relevant and relatable gay representation on screen for adults. But there was still no programming for children.

In the UK, there have been a few, limited examples of LGBT characters appearing in teen targeted shows, such as *Hollyoaks*, in particular the John Paul and Craig storyline. For the past 30 years, there have been both positively scripted and negatively scripted LGBT storylines from some of the mainstream soaps, like

EastEnders, *Emmerdale* and *Coronation Street*. A soap that really hit the headlines back in 1994 was *Brookside*, with the series being the first to air a kiss between two female characters pre-watershed. In the same year, the BBC's *Byker Grove* became the first children's British drama to broach the subject of "coming out of the closet" when Noddy Fishwick kissed his close friend Gary Hendrix at the back of a cinema. These storylines were so important to the young fans who watched them as they gave many the confidence to talk openly about their sexuality and provided on-screen characters that they could identify with. Since then, there have been many shows across the globe that have had LGBT characters and storylines, but there are still few LGBT lead characters. Now, the explosion of YouTubers and digital media has created new ways for kids to see relatable and relevant content. LGBT representation in kids' television remains a new area for commercial media.

Disney Channel's LGBT Storylines

Globally, Disney Channel made history of its own in 2014 with the inclusion of same sex parents in an episode of *Good Luck Charlie*. Each of the parents meet "a" mum of Charlie's new friend Taylor, and realise they have met two different women – Taylor's two mums. The episode was crafted with the assistance of the organisation known as GLAAD, a media organisation dedicated to combating and dispelling negative stereotypes of LGBT people in the media. The initial airing of the episode was met with opposition, but it has aired throughout the world since then.

In early 2017, Disney Junior aired an episode of animated hit *Doc McStuffins*, which was praised by GLAAD for being "groundbreaking" and featured an interracial lesbian couple, voiced by Wanda Sykes and Portia De Rossi. Commenting on the episode titled *The Emergency Plan*, creator Chris Nee said "I always envision *Doc McStuffins* as a show about what it means to accept everyone as part of our communities. As part of a two-mom family, I'm proud to have an episode that reflects my son's world, and shows everyone that love is love in McStuffinsville."

In my current role as VP of Production for Disney Channels EMEA, we had an opportunity to re-make the Israeli format *North Star*, re-titled *The Lodge*. We adapted the tween soap-like drama and took the basic story of a girl (Skye) moving to her family's lodge in the country, adding new characters as well as music and dance. One of the new characters was Josh, Skye's best friend back in the city. As we developed him, we saw an opportunity to create a gay character – which would be the first ever for a Disney-branded live action show produced in EMEA. We decided to address the storyline in the second season.

In prepping how to handle the storyline, we weighed various options with the writer and creative team. We were evolving the plots of the overall season, and felt we didn't necessarily have the scope to include romantic storylines for Josh just yet. But we did want him to acknowledge his sexuality, and created a scene in the third episode when Josh is catching up with Noah, who is missing his unrequited love, Kaylee, in the city. Noah asks Josh how he and Skye keep up their long-distance friendship, and then asks why Josh and Skye never dated. It is in this scene, that Josh says that he is not into girls "in that way".

The creation of the scene and the dialogue were specifically crafted to show a few things. We wanted to show a character who was confident in who he was, and not afraid to be honest with one of his friends. We chose Noah to be able to model, for boys, a way to accept differences in others, as his reaction is mildly surprised, but quickly accepting. *The Lodge* episode premiered across UK and in around 100 countries across EMEA and received strong support from viewers and fans.

In 2018, LGBT storylines were taken to a new level with Disney Channel series *Andi Mack*, which airs in the UK, and across the world. The series is executive-produced by Terri Minsky and is currently in its second season in the UK. The second season began with the revelation of Cyrus questioning his sexuality and eventually acknowledging he has feelings for Jonah, the main character's romantic interest. This realisation begins an important part of his journey to self-discovery as a gay individual and ultimately, his self-acceptance. The storyline has received positive support from viewers and the media with Vogue.com reporting that the announcement "serves as another step towards content for kids that is informed by reality". The series has also improved its rating performance since the episode aired.

For both *Andi Mack* and *The Lodge,* Disney worked with GLAAD to ensure the

Andi Mack

messaging was on point and appropriate for the audience. We also worked closely with the actors to ensure their performances were genuine and considered. Disney went on to win the inaugural Kids Content Award at the GLAAD Awards for *Andi Mack*, and was nominated by the British LGBT Awards – both for the media moment for Andi Mack and for myself as a Top 10 Diversity Champion.

Summary

Why is it important for LGBT characters to be represented in kids' TV? It is important that every young person should feel included by seeing a version of themselves on screen. Our characters go on personal journeys, and are in the process of figuring themselves out. Both Cyrus and Josh are at different points in their journeys, allowing different children to react differently. It is important that both children and parents watch something that they are not only entertained by, but engaged by. This might initiate a conversation between parent and child that invites the parent to ask "Has that ever happened to you?"

As an industry, we have come a long way over the past 30 years. However, there is still a way to go and so many more important stories to tell. As creators of content targeted at young people, we are in a fantastic position. We can use the power of television and the internet to entertain, with inspirational and aspirational themes that demonstrate the diverse world we live in, and provide characters that are relatable and reflective of *all* of our audiences.

SMALL PEOPLE, BIG PICTURE

ALLANAH LANGSTAFF

———

"I can't wait to grow up" is a sentence almost every child and teenager utters at some point in their life, while adults scoff and remind them about how lucky they are to be free from the responsibilities of our adult world. But no matter how much we try and shield children from the banality and stress of adult life, there are bigger picture issues that can't be hidden from them. Children have access to information at their fingertips and their curious nature means they will seek out answers when adults tell them something is none of their concern. As content producers, the challenge for us is how we reflect their world and accept their awareness without diluting the pure joy of being a child and without sacrificing entertainment values.

We live in a world where the environment these children will inherit is constantly under threat, where lawmakers push back on legislation to halt school shootings, where innocent children enjoying an Ariana Grande concert are targets of terrorism, and where more than 30% of British children live in poverty. Adults don't need to tell children about these issues; they are living them.

So, what can we do, and how do we acknowledge that the world children live in isn't perfect without dumping our fears and worries on them through the entertainment they watch?

Last summer I had the joy of working on my first CBeebies series, *Junk Rescue*, which premiered on World Environment Day. The series celebrated artisanal craft and sustainability, subjects which can sometimes be a bit dry for adult audiences, but paired with the limitless imagination of the children who took part, it was a lesson in not being constrained by the zeitgeist and what other people think. In the series, children saw incredible transformations to pieces of junk most commonly shoved in the boot and taken to the dump – think scraps of wooden furniture, torn sofa cushions, old clothes. The artisan craftspeople used skills honed from years of practice to transform junk into beautiful and useful pieces for the junkyard, and the kids were truly captivated by the transformation that took place. Meanwhile, the kids used junk they found and collected from the junkyard to make their own objects – it was child-led play which saw all manner of items created from bird play houses to thrones.

As the children saw it, they had made useful and beautiful objects which slotted into the play world they create for themselves. To them, where the junk came from wasn't the concern, it was how they could manipulate the materials they had to work with to fit in with their ideas. They weren't limited by the practicalities, and sustainability wasn't presented as a problem to them that they had to fix, rather, it was an opportunity – here was a load of FREE material that they could use to make whatever they wanted. The adult's role was that of facilitator to help them execute those ideas, without telling them what to do or sidelining the children's outlandish plans for something "recognisable". It was a real lesson for us in trusting our audience and contributors by taking away an element of producer control. The outcome was incredibly satisfying and worthwhile to see, knowing children at home don't always have access to elaborate craft kits but almost always have access to "junk".

Junk Rescue

Sustainability for the CBeebies audience seems like a relatively low risk subject to tackle, but it encompasses politics and commercialism in a way that isn't preachy or makes you feel hopeless in the face of it. Public service broadcasting is in the privileged position of having a duty to create this type of content with a remit to make sure there are the slots to show it. But what about more commercial opportunities? How do we tackle themes that seem more adult in content yet affect younger audiences, topics they want to know more about? We need to move the conversation forward and look at the wider issue of attributing "wokeness" to an audience, as invariably this concept can come from a place of privilege. Our content should try and be inclusive of all audience members and speak to a universal audience, but how do we do that while recognising that some children are living these issues, while others are observing them? It's a big topic and it's going to take our collective knowledge to forge new pathways for a growing audience in an ever changing world. ◐

SCREWBALL!

BOB AYRES

——

In 2017, our online schools channel TrueTube made a short comedy drama called *Screwball!* to help teachers open up discussion in Relationships and Sex Education (RSE) lessons. The film met with critical acclaim and has won several awards in the year since its release, but the film's genesis began a long, long time ago...

Cue wibbly flashback effect:

"... and Bob, you're doing sex education."

"Why do I get sex education?"

"Because you're used to discussing sex and stuff."

This was ten years ago. I was still a teacher, and at that moment I was sitting in a Year 8 form tutors meeting while the Head of Year decided who would teach what during the coming term's PSHE lessons. That's Personal, Social, Health and Economic education, since you ask. Steve got drugs and alcohol, Baldeep got bullying, I got sex education...

"You talk about it all the time in RE."

Yes, I taught Religious Education (a great conversation stopper at parties, by the way) and yes, I did discuss sex and relationships with my students, but in the context of What Religions Teach About Pre-Marital Sex, Contraception And Abortion, And Why They Disapprove Of Pretty Much All Of That Kind Of Thing.

I sighed. But, I supposed, better me than the Art teacher over there who got pregnant by a member of the PE department (I have changed their departments in order to protect their identities. Or have I?).

Actually, Sex Ed. turned out to be a lot of fun: I got to do the "how to put a condom on" lesson using the school's collection of battered blue plastic penises (hilarious!), and the STI lesson with plastic cups of water, starch solution and iodine (it would take too long to explain). And during the course of teaching nearly 200 13-year-olds about chlamydia, gonorrhoea and other difficult-to-spell words, I realised how vital Relationships and Sex Education is. The blind ignorance that some of the young people had about their own bodies was shocking (e.g. some girls not knowing what a period was), and the astonishing myths that some of them believed about sex (e.g. "You won't get pregnant if you do it standing up") would have been funny if they weren't so potentially risky.

The young people at my school were lucky to have RSE on their timetables, because it isn't compulsory in all schools.

At present, only schools under the

Screwball!

control of their local authority have to teach RSE, which means that academies, free schools, and independent schools are all exempt. But in March 2017, the then Education Secretary Justine Greening announced that RSE was to be compulsory in all English schools from September 2019.

Obviously, not everyone is pleased about this. A lot of people, often religious people, feel that it is a family's place to teach their children what they need to know about sex. But from what I was told by the young people in my lessons, that kind of teaching is often just, "Don't do it until you're married", which isn't big on the kind of detail that might be useful to a young person confused or even frightened by the images they've just seen on their friend's phone.

Part of the worry is that children will be told or shown things in RSE lessons that aren't appropriate for their age. A lot of this is just good old-fashioned prudery, but it also shows a lack of trust in the professionalism of teachers. Age appropriateness is something I thought about a lot when teaching the condom lesson to my Year 8s. I was fully aware that in any one class, I would have never-been-kissed teenagers sitting next to their sexually active peers.

Then there's the belief that if you tell young people about sex, they're immediately going to go and do it. Actually, research shows that if young people have had good RSE lessons, they are more likely to delay having sex for the first time, and more likely to take precautions when they finally do.

And of course, some parents don't want extra-marital or same-sex relationships presented as "normal". But take a look around – "normal" certainly isn't one man with one woman for life. If someone wants to teach that as an "ideal" to aim for in their family, then that's entirely up to them, but their children are eventually going to learn about a whole variety of other ways to be. Surely it's better for them to be taught about sex and relationships by a responsible adult in a safe environment, rather than through online porn, or (possibly distressing) experience?

Nevertheless, parents will retain the right to remove their children from RSE lessons under the new legislation. And in Wales, Scotland and Northern Ireland, the law isn't changing at all.

For those young people who remain in their freshly compulsory RSE lessons, the question of what and how to teach them is still looming. RSE is often delivered by teachers of other subjects who have been handed a folder of worksheets (if they are lucky) and told to get on with it. The government's last guidance on the subject was published in 2000, and this was back in the Dark Ages before the ubiquitous smartphone and before the word "sexting" had passed into common parlance. Presumably, the government will provide new guidelines before September 2019, but in the meantime, a variety of organisations are stepping in to help fill the vacuum with advice and resources of their own.

"We are not putting explicit sex on TrueTube!"

A little context here: this was in early 2017, and I was now the Head of TrueTube – an online platform that makes free short films for schools, and (later that year) winner of the Children's BAFTA for Channel of the Year, not that I like to go on about it. I was having a meeting with Adam Tyler who was going to direct an RSE film for the site, and during our discussion about content, he suggested that we put a

"positive representation of real, loving sex" on the TrueTube servers.

We wanted to cram as many important issues into the film as possible: consent, peer pressure, body image, sexting, the detrimental influence of online porn … quite a big ask for a ten-minute film, but we were keen to give it a go. The conversation with Adam had moved on to what we could and couldn't show, and what we could and couldn't say. Adam was all for completely ignoring traditional British reserve about, you know… um … sex; I was thinking of the classroom context in which the film would eventually be shown. The film was to be aimed at the 13–16 age group, but we didn't want teens to feel talked down to (adults make themselves look stupid when they treat children like they're stupid). It had to be entertaining and irreverent enough to hold their attention while being detailed enough to say what it needed to without pulling punches. But it couldn't be so explicit that it wouldn't get past the gatekeepers: the teachers. Teachers aren't going to stand at the front of a class and show something that will make them cringe or put them in an awkward position. And they certainly don't want the kids to go home and describe to their parents what they watched at school today if there's even a whiff of unsuitability. Our film had to be something teachers would want to use.

But, most importantly, it had to face the honest truth about the world in which young people are now living. And it's a very different world from the one their parents (and their teachers) grew up in. When I was 11, a boy came into school brandishing a copy of the *Sun* and, of course, all his friends gathered round to get a good look at page 3. These days they'd be gathering round a smartphone to watch something far more graphic. According to a Middlesex University study, 28% of 11–12-year-olds have seen explicit material online, and 65% of 15–16-year-olds. And those are the ones who will admit to it.

In mainstream media, most depictions of sex are misleading. Not what I would call educational at all, although I realise that's rarely the point. Sex is often completely offscreen, so we learn that it's something furtive and dirty. Or it's onscreen but we learn that it's best performed to a soft rock track in a series of awkward tableaux, particular body parts hidden under artfully draped sheets. And there shouldn't be any talking.

So, young people are turning to online porn to satisfy their curiosity, but what they see is just as misrepresentative and likely to be much more harmful, giving young people the impression that sex is all about male gratification, and by any means necessary.

And in most representations of sex across all media, the "relationship" bit of "sexual relationship" gets left out altogether.

Taking all this into account, Adam performed an impressive balancing act in writing his script. He took inspiration from the "screwball" comedy genre of the '30s and '40s with its smart rapid-fire dialogue and moments of slapstick humour to tell a story about two extremely talkative 17-year-olds preparing to have sex for the first time. They have to deal with the massive gaps

in their knowledge, the misinformation they've picked up from online porn, their own insecurities and – *spoiler alert* – cats. In talking things through, instead of getting on with any actual sex, they get a better understanding of themselves and each other and ultimately develop a much healthier relationship … and so model good behaviour for our young audience.

Screwball! – the finished film – was gleefully received by teachers and the RSE community, and given rapturous applause when we screened it at the Sex Education Forum's (SEF) annual conference last summer.

Adam won the Writer award at the Children's BAFTAs 2017; and both of our young actors – Alhaji Fofana and Savannah Baker – were nominated for the Performer award, with Alhaji eventually taking home the trophy (Savannah wasn't too disappointed).

Screwball!'s reception proves that there is a hunger for good RSE resources in the lead up to September 2019, and an opportunity for filmmakers to tell stories for the 13–16 age group that feature the real lives and concerns of young people on the brink of adulthood.

I will finish with a quote from the SEF Conference where, after we'd screened *Screwball!*, a very respectable-looking lady in her 60s, with grey hair, horn-rimmed glasses and a smart floral-print dress, stood up and said,

"It was so refreshing to see a film that wasn't all about penetration!" ◯

LET'S HEAR IT FOR THE GIRLS

BETH PARKER

—

Recent news storms and the #MeToo campaign have made it very clear that we have some way to go before we can say we have achieved gender parity in the entertainment industry. These issues have to be dealt with at a societal level as well as at an industry level. But with both, perhaps the way to address bad behaviour is to demonstrate how good behaviour works to the benefit of all.

From where I'm sitting (and granted, that is a privileged position), the animation industry has seen marked change for the better in recent years. So, instead of wagging our fingers at our male peers, maybe we should be celebrating those women who succeed in this business, of which there are many, while ensuring those coming through the ranks feel empowered and supported to follow their dreams. Where there has indeed been change, we must remember that centuries of patriarchal conditioning still make us question our abilities and worth. It is this conditioning as well as the "conditioners" that need challenging. For example, can we please stop saying "we can be just as good as them"? Being a man is not the benchmark for greatness; it's being the best you can be, whoever you are.

One of the first animators was a German woman called Lotte Reiniger. She was beavering away on her 1926 feature film *The Adventures of Prince Achmed*, not a million miles away from where Käthe Kollwitz was completing her famous anti-war posters of 1924. Some sixty years previous, Julia Margaret Cameron was given her first camera with which she produced some of the most exquisitely beautiful portraits ever taken. The work these women produced stands out to me, because it is not only wonderful, but is so very different to that of their male contemporaries. Despite working at a time when white men controlled all domains of life, these women did not try to compete by expressing themselves as men did, but instead embraced their female point of view. With that came a warmth we all recognise from our sisters, mothers and grandmothers – something that could be said to be uniquely female.

These women were not celebrated anywhere near as much as they should have been in their own lifetimes, if indeed they were celebrated at all. But more and more of us are now discovering their work and that of women like them, and are being inspired to follow suit. It is this energy and progress that also inspires the founding of networks such as Animated Women UK (AWUK) to ensure businesses like ours don't lose the rich variation of perspective all genders can bring.

AWUK covers both the animation and VFX sectors. We have five pillars:

- Networking is the simplest way to empower women – nothing can help a career more than the right contacts, so we provide the space for women to make those connections.

- Mentoring is something which can benefit mentors as much as mentees, so programmes such as the Helen North Achieve Programme enable women to support one another, regardless of the amount of experience they have in the business.

- Showcasing members enables us to celebrate women in our business. Giving women a platform to talk about their career journeys gives them confidence while inspiring others.

- Recruitment is where we can ensure women get a fair deal. Working with industry partners, we can ensure opportunities are open to all and that the workplace is free of harassment and discrimination.

- Education is where it all starts. From those who don't even know there is a career to be had in animation, to those who have chosen this business, but don't know where to start; our aim is to support women at the very beginning of their careers in the animation and VFX industries.

Women have always been the builders of communities and that is very much our ethos at AWUK. We are a community of practice where ideas, concerns and sometimes just general chat are all shared – we all put in as much as we take out.

As we celebrate the centenary of women's suffrage here in the UK, it is worth remembering the genuine progress that has been made, whilst not forgetting the steps we still need to take. For too long the world has been run by cisgender white males and we have many steps still to take before all perspectives are considered of equal value. In this business, diversity and inclusion are only achieved if the content we produce represents the varied world we live in and is made by all those who live here. ◯

CHILDREN'S RADIO

KAYLEIGH KEAM

There's no OBE after my name. I'm not a commissioner, an executive or a BAFTA winner. I'm not even a producer. Until six months ago I was a researcher. So how, then, do I have over 100 scripts on my CV? How did a researcher come to write series after series of top end brands such as *Something Special, Tree Fu Tom* and *The Furchester Hotel*? The answer is simple. Children's radio.

In our media industry, it is not uncommon for people to have grassroots in local radio. A "lowly" broadcast assistant just answers phones and prints running orders, right? Wrong.

For those of you like me, who started your media career in local radio, you will know how "hands on" your role can be in actually producing content. Smaller teams and inevitably smaller budgets see you driving the desk, being packed off with a microphone to interview a local MP or cutting packages together for the Breakfast Show. The same goes for the lesser known world of children's radio (minus the local MP).

In a world dominated by new and emerging visual content, it is never a surprise to me to see young children "looking" for the voice talking to them from a podcast. Children are less familiar with digesting content through *listening* alone. Yet, there is a wealth of children's audio programming available that not only entertains and educates, but can equip children with the vital skill of active listening.

As content creators for children, we all know the crucial role that listening skills, creativity and imagination play in a child's development. The National Curriculum acknowledges that they contribute to "*the development of social, intellectual, physical and communication skills, children's confidence and self-esteem*".

Despite being low down in the pecking order of the media world, working as a researcher in children's radio opened doors

that would have been locked for many years had I been working at the same level in television.

Being able to write for internationally known characters such as Elmo was an absolute honour. But creating audio content for pre-schoolers without any visual stimulus isn't without its challenges. Children's radio programmes have no impressive studio sets and no beautifully crafted animation. How, then, do you hold the attention of a pre-schooler without any hint of visual stimulus? My younger writing self would cram every second with dialogue and action because, *how else could I keep them focused?* It wasn't until I started to observe children listening to shows that I realised I was completely missing the mark. My shows didn't need endless dialogue, they needed pauses. They needed breathing space. If we are providing children with the soundscapes and characters to paint pictures in their own minds, they need the space to actually paint them. Pauses are crucial, even at the highest jeopardy point. Extend the music bed, push back the next line of voice-over, let children *imagine* the world you are creating for them.

Audio content gives a child's imagination complete ownership in the same way that reading a book does. When we read, we imagine characters' expressions, picture the colours, visualise the world that the author creates. How often has this imagined world been so vivid that you feel crushing dissatisfaction at seeing your perfectly imagined protagonist on screen for the first time? *She looks nothing like I imagined*.

My dad always maintained it was more exciting to *listen* to a football match than to watch it. The break in a commentator's voice as a goal is scored, the roar of stadium cheers, the sound of

drums banging in the crowd … would you notice these if you were just watching?

I had never written a script in my life prior to working in children's radio. I'd never made a programme. I'd never written a poem or a story. Why would I have? I'd only been in the industry for a year or so. Yet just like my first few months at BBC Radio Cambridgeshire, I was catapulted into the deep end. Scripts needed writing, programmes needed editing.

Five years after being asked to "just have a go" at writing a radio script, I have discovered that I **absolutely love** writing for children. So much so that I recently took the plunge to go part-time and write a children's book.

So, if you, like me, are on the lower rungs of your media career ladder, I cannot encourage you enough to explore the world of children's radio. Discover what is out there, shout about it, play it to little listeners. Never written in your life? Have a go at writing a radio script – go on, I dare you.

Never underestimate this lesser known platform and the effect it has on children.

Never underestimate the impact that it can have on your career. ◉

Mr Owl, Studio Hari

MAKING YOUR FANS FALL IN LOVE WITH YOUR CONTENT

HELEN DUGDALE

Once the last word is written, the final illustration is complete and the animator has finished working their magic, the journey to tell the world about your great content begins.

- **Time to call a friend.** It's now time to pick up the phone and get in contact with everyone you know in the countries that you're trying to break into. As the old adage goes, "if you don't ask, you don't get", so start reaching out. Ask if anyone knows a journalist, writer or blogger who is well connected and could help make some key introductions or cover your story in the countries you're wanting to crack.

- **Step outside your network.** Tap into the power of industry networks, bodies and foundations across the UK and the countries that your content is heading for. They'll have websites, social media, blogs, newsletters, and (maybe) even printed marketing material that you can write for. They are usually on the look-out for content.

- **What's the one unique thing about your story?** The one thing that makes your content different? When you find that hook, it needs to run through every part of your media and PR campaign.

- **Get the parents onside.** Making kids fall in love with your content and characters is essential. But you also need to win over the busy, sometimes weary grown-ups who don't really want to part with any more cash to download that app, buy the game or that piece of merchandise. They need to know what's so great about your content or your show that means they should let their children spend time with your characters. What can you do to win them over? Can you use your campaign to appeal to them using humour, irony, or wit? Or maybe you could appeal to them by picking up on the same frustrations parents face the world over.

- **Has something similar been done before?** Can you ride on the coat tails of a previous show or game that is similar to yours? Is there a similar book, toy or another show that has found a winning formula, enjoyed a strong relationship with its target audience and/or made friends with the media?

Little Lunch, Gristmill Productions

- **Are you reaching for mass appeal or a niche targeted list of journalists?** If you're announcing something or making an official statement, a press release may be the best vehicle to kick-start your campaign. If you're wanting to comment on a trend or on news in relation to your brand, a personalised pitch may be best. There are many PR tools to help you tell your story.
- **Understand cultural references.** Make it a priority to get to know each country. It's about drilling down and understanding the relevance for each market you're targeting. It's not enough to just translate a press release; each country needs its own spin or angle.

- **Can you partner with an international brand?** It doesn't need to be as flashy and expensive as it sounds. Could one of your characters take over a social media channel for a complimentary brand? Maybe answer questions on social media? This could take place simultaneously in different countries for maximum impact.
- **Is there a relevant international day or week you can hijack?** Can you lock in your launch at the same time as an international day or week? Maybe partner with a charity or brand that already has activity planned? https://www.awarenessdays.com/awareness-days-calendar/category/international-awareness/.
- **Go and meet your audience.** Step out from behind the comfort of the digital world and go and meet your audience. You want to know them as much as they want to know you. You can't just rely on trailers, posters or tweets. You need face-to-face time with your future fans. Actually meeting your audiences where they are, and contributing to their passions and experiences in real life, goes a long way. Good luck. ◌

Mr. Carton, Michaël Bolufer & Fabien Daphy, Tant Mieux Prod

KIDS ON EARTH – THE NEXT NORMAL

HOWARD BLUMENTHAL

—

Five key ideas are shaping our next generation:

- Half of the world's children and teenagers are literate and connected through technology, with another quarter not far behind.
- Video is taking the place of print and writing as our primary means of sharing ideas.
- Informal education among peers is overwhelming the limitations of school and formal learning.
- Children and teenagers are learning what they want to learn, when they want to learn, and how much they want to learn.
- Global citizenship is disrupting local, regional, state, provincial, and national thinking.

As Alejandra in Massachusetts waits patiently for Danilo in the Philippines to wake up and play Minecraft before she goes to bed, Alej is on FaceTime with her sister Maria in Mexico, and asks to see the new Australian Shepherd puppy. Maria tells her sister about Li Wei, whose parents are Chinese (dad) and Egyptian (mum). He says he's Chigyptian. Alej thinks he's cute.

As nationalist politics enjoys its last blast of power, localism faces a big challenge. People are no longer living the lives they once did. In many classrooms, kids with roots in Kenya or Greece sit next to kids from Brazil and Vietnam, and become friends. They read books by Roald Dahl and J. K. Rowling. They watch Nickelodeon. They know Ariana Grande's concert was bombed in Manchester, England, and that she returned for a benefit show. They like to eat pizza and fried chicken, pasta and Chinese food, too. The new normal isn't just international – connecting one country to another – it's global.

It doesn't matter whether they're 8 or 15 – kids are curious. The internet has opened a new world for them, a world they can explore by making friends everywhere. Well aware of potential dangers, and quite reasonably assuming adults are hard at work to keep them safe, children and teenagers watch and listen to far away people and places. They ask questions and, sometimes, those questions are answered. Little of this is structured, well-researched, properly supervised, or responsibly monitored, but that's not going to stop an 11-year-old who wants to learn more about kangaroos or the royal wedding.

Years ago, I created and produced a popular television series called *Where in the World Is Carmen Sandiego?* for PBS in the USA and several other countries. We developed *Carmen* by talking to over a thousand children in the US, asking them what they knew about the world and what they wanted to know. Recently, I started that process again, talking to kids in schools in the U.S. and then around the world.

When an NGO offered a Media Fellowship to interview children and teenagers in Uganda last summer, I realised how little I knew about a country with 43 million people. Most US adults knew as little as I did (vague 1970s references to Entebbe and Idi Amin). Kids in the US were uncertain whether Uganda was a country, an article of clothing, or a kind of animal.

I visited four schools in Uganda. The children and teenagers were very proud of their "peaceful nation". Well aware of Uganda's struggles with corruption and poor economic opportunity, they were studying to become doctors, members of parliament, teachers, and engineers. They knew a lot about US politics – parsing key achievements in Obama's presidency, expressing high hopes for Trump (because

his decisions affect everyone in the world), explaining how and why Clinton lost the 2016 election. How do they know all of this? Television and dinner table conversation, but mostly the internet.

Under the protection of "no question is a stupid question", I asked about wild animals in Africa. Do they roam the streets of Kampala, the capital city of Uganda? Do local students ever walk beside a giraffe on the way to school? Their answers were good-humoured (being silly plays well in just about every country). No, they explained (with a smile on their faces), those animals live in the safety of the savannah up north, in a game park. They became comfortable asking their own questions. Few had travelled beyond Uganda, except, perhaps, on a school trip to nearby Kenya or Tanzania.

When I told them I was travelling to Hong Kong next, they asked about food, school, climate, football (soccer), families, China, ferry boats, language, pets, houses, subways, and more. I was curious, too, not only about life in Hong Kong, but about how, exactly, I would cause local kids in Hong Kong to magically appear before me, with personal release forms signed by parents, to be recorded by a video camera and a microphone that I did not yet own or know how to operate. Thank goodness for the internet, email, and the kindness of strangers!

The kids I encountered at a school for musical theatre in Hong Kong were informal and articulate. Their parents came from Korea, the Netherlands, Germany, Australia, New Zealand, and the United

States, always with a mum from one place and a dad from another. Trips to visit relatives on other continents were common. Unlike Uganda, where most people's roots extend from rural villages to Kampala for job and educational opportunities, the sense in Hong Kong was not international, but global. The entire world was available to those with the interest and inclination to explore and make the necessary connections.

Thilo was co-starring in a very large (and fun!) musical comedy called *Priscilla: Queen of the Desert*. There were posters for the show everywhere in Hong Kong's MTR public transport system. Speaking like a seasoned performer, the 12-year-old casually told me about his character's role in the story of two drag queens and a transgender woman (Priscilla is a lavender-coloured bus on its way to Alice Springs). He was so nonchalant about the subject matter – and I wondered whether I would meet other kids, in other parts of the world, whose parents would be so open-minded. And when the time came, how would I start a discussion with a ten-year-old about faith and religion, knowing that the video would be shown throughout the world on a Kids on Earth website or Vimeo channel?

Next stop was a proper boy's school in Altrincham, near Manchester, England. Those young men were well-mannered, dressed like the private school students I met in Uganda (also, British Empire). Still, they were running around the schoolyard, tagging and teasing, tossing balls around, huddling with groups of friends, easily distracted, just like boys

and girls everywhere in the world. As we settled down for one-on-one interviews, I found out that Kylan's dad was a British football star originally from Barbados; Franek told me about his extended family in Poland. Like the US, England is now very international, rich with immigrants.

Moving on, I was less certain about the students I would encounter in an upscale suburban middle school outside Philadelphia. This year's American football champions – the Super Bowl winners – were the Philadelphia Eagles, so I was prepared for young teenage fans wearing Eagles sweatshirts. I did not anticipate chatting about shopping malls in Ulan Bator with Olivia, who had recently relocated from Mongolia, nor did I expect to meet Sianna, a joyful fourteen-year-old who is helping to raise four foster children in a family with financial challenges. I met kids from Moldova, Israel, Ukraine, India, Russia, and Japan. They were media savvy, knowledgeable about healthy food (often preferring less healthy options), good students if not quite as dedicated or diligent as those I met in Uganda, frequent travellers to nearby ocean beaches and New York City (about two hours away). They do their homework, love and tangle with siblings, bicycle around the neighbourhood, read, learn to cook, and play outside with friends. Some play video games, but only a few were interested in pop culture, movies, or TV.

Next, I am off to Bulgaria, then Slovenia, then England for our conference, hopeful about a side trip to Scotland or Wales. There are whispers about travels to the Philippines, Uruguay, and southern

Australia later this year. This summer, we'll try something new: interviews conducted by a professor and undergraduates as part of a project in Sierra Leone. A musician and producer in Pakistan and a graduate student in Afghanistan who is addressing kids' concerns about terrorism, have also volunteered to record local interviews to our specifications. In connection with global citizenship and the United Nations Sustainable Development Goals, some students are planning to record their own Kids on Earth interviews in their primary and middle schools. Later this year, we'll begin to explore other languages, translations and captions (in part to understand non-English speakers, in part to familiarise young people with languages other than their own). We will begin to record interviews via Skype, careful not to sacrifice informality or authenticity in the process. We are beginning to work with children who require assistive devices to communicate, with young people in refugee families, and in remote locations, including, perhaps, central Alaska and Appalachia. We are collaborating with university professors on research projects related to authentic storytelling, often within their specialities, including public health, journalism, international law, and developmental psychology.

Every day, we think in terms of three steps: awareness through storytelling, connected kids, and altruism.

Kids on Earth storytelling is authentic and simple, very lightly produced, gently directed and minimally edited. There is no merchandising or licensing programme, but someday, maybe a lot of young people will wear Kids on Earth caps or t-shirts, or carry books in a Kids on Earth backpack (books sent by young friends in other countries where books are abundant). Right now, we're raising awareness – it's tough to care about somebody if you've never heard of the country they live in.

Over two billion kids live on earth. If we could provide a safe way to connect every one of them, that's what we would do. For now, we participate in public policy discussions to assure a future of secure connections to promote curiosity and global understanding.

We believe kids are naturally compassionate, happy to help one another. We're meeting potential partners to develop 21st century programmes for public good, powered by the first connected, literate generation of global citizens.

You can help in three ways. First, introduce us to schools and teachers around the world. Second, connect us with resources to expand our travel budget so we can interview more children and teenagers around the world. Third, when you're seeking a partner passionate about global citizenship for young people, please keep us in mind. ○

To learn more about Kids on Earth, please visit: www.kidsonearth.org

To watch a lot of Kids on Earth videos, go to: https://vimeo.com/user31644857

Wharton article: http://knowledge.wharton.upenn.edu/article/how-the-next-generation-of-global-kids-will-learn-from-one-another/

About Howard Blumenthal: http://www.hblumenthal.com

Gudrun: The Viking Princess

HISTORY, NATURAL HISTORY, VIKINGS AND THEIR ANIMALS!

NIGEL POPE

The Story of *Gudrun: the Viking Princess*

As someone who's worked in the fields of natural history and children's programming for their entire TV career, I've always wanted to try and create something which brought these two wonderful worlds together. Way back in the late 1990s in Bristol, I'd produced *The Really Wild Show* and lots of other presenter-led animal shows, but since setting up Maramedia, the Glasgow-based Indie in 2011, that goal had always eluded our small but endlessly creative core team comprising myself, director-cameraman Justin Purefoy, producer Jackie Savery, researcher Fiona Donaldson, composer Fraser Purdie and editor Pete Barden.

Often we'd brainstorm new formats and concepts, auditioning new presenters and shooting tasters, but the results always fell short or lacked freshness. Then one November day in late 2016, we found ourselves pitching to CBeebies controller Kay Benbow. It was a good session but there were no instant "holes in one". However, just before leaving we had time for a good old telly gossip and I told Kay about our new slate of commissions which included a wildlife programme about the Viking North. Suddenly a few random thoughts connected and I found myself spontaneously suggesting a series of shorts about the wild adventures of a Viking Prince, narrated by a leading Scottish actor (of course!). A mad idea, but it might just work! And one slight amendment from Kay. It should be a girl – a Viking princess!

Within a couple of months we had our pilot commissioned and with all the key talent already signed up for our main natural history Viking epic, wc were good to go.

I suppose it hadn't really occurred to me that wrangling a cast of child and adult actors in period dress, a menagerie of live animals, and reproduction Viking ships and forts on a relatively limited budget was quite a challenge! We all pressed on, though, with huge faith in our mission to create a series of little stories connecting our young heroine Gudrun (played by young local actress Sophie Ryder) and her friends to the ways of the wild.

So, on a savagely cold day in March 2017, the team found itself in the wildly romantic location of Alladale wilderness reserve in Sutherland. This estate owned by philanthropist Paul Lister is the location for an ongoing project to re-wild Scotland with wolves, bears, lynx and elk! Paul is still working on that one, but we were definitely ready for action with our top team.

Pete (drone op as well as editor), Justin, Fiona and myself were now joined by Sophie, Johnny McGuinness as King Sigurd, top falconer Lloyd Buck, wildlife camera ace John Waters and at the heart of it all Lloyd's beautiful gyrfalcon, Isla, in the role of Freya.

The weather threw everything at us, of course. We had snow showers, sleet, sunshine, mist and clear blue skies all within 48 hours. But despite the adversity something seemed to click. It felt different and fresh and suddenly everyone had bought in to the concept in the most passionate way you could imagine.

Back in Glasgow, Pete and I set to work on the edit. By now Julia Bond had been appointed as our commissioning exec and I'd agreed to show her and Kay the completed pilot in a week! As edits go, this was one of the best ever – Justin and Pete's images mixing beautifully with John

Waters' slo-mo falcon material shot at 800fps on a 4K Phantom flex camera.

For the narration, I'd been inspired by a recent Nat Geo wildlife series from Icon Films in Bristol called *Savage Kingdom*, voiced by Charles Dance. It hadn't been everyone's cup of tea, but I loved the way that the narrator addressed the characters in a direct way – prompting and commenting on their actions, slipping in advice, warnings and praise! This seemed a good way to go for *The Viking Princess*. So, I quickly drafted a script along these lines and Fraser Purdie dreamed up a delicious score seemingly within the space of a day!

The viewing with Julia and Kay went well, I think, as the series was commissioned on the spot and at the time of writing we're actually editing the second series.

Gudrun: The Viking Princess

Gudrun: The Viking Princess

I was also lucky enough to be able to bring former Head of Children's for BBC Scotland, Simon Parsons, into the mix after the shooting of the pilot. At the time of writing we've now created stories with 19 different animal species with Simon at the helm. I hope we can do more.

The team is really proud of Gudrun. Connecting children with the natural world is so important in this age of ever-multiplying devices and platforms and in our little episodes it does feel like we've addressed this very 21st century issue with a good set of ethics straight from the 10th century!

FAMILY MATTERS

TOM O'CONNELL

I'm lucky enough to be entering the second year of my Three Arrows journey, working alongside the talented and enormously supportive double act of Jon Hancock and David Hallam. Earlier this year we launched *Treasure Champs* on CBeebies, a colourful mix of animation, story dramatisations and child-led content making abstract values understandable in a way that is meaningful to 4–6-year-olds. We're hugely proud of the series and the amazing team of people who brought it to life. I couldn't be happier to be a continuing member of the Three Arrows family!

Family is absolutely key to what Three Arrows is all about, from the warm, inclusive working environment Jon and Dave have created (and in the early days, this environment *was* the Hancock family home!) to their belief in a shared family experience when watching TV. As a dad, I've seen first-hand how children's telly can shape the worlds of our audience. I passionately believe that kids' TV works best when it serves as a jumping off point for family discussion, when it inspires real world experiences for our viewers.

CBeebies and CBBC are packed with series that are ripe for this sort of family exploration, from *Andy's Wild Adventures* to *Do You Know*? and the enduring and pretty incredible *Horrible Histories* – in my opinion a near perfect Reithian product!

Children like watching stuff with *other* people. In our house they might, more often than not, be huddled around a tablet instead of the TV set, but they're huddled together, and they're talking about the things they're watching (whilst being properly supervised, of course).

But to engage families we should understand that our audience's experiences of what a "family" actually is are as diverse and unique as they are. Children's series including *The Dumping Ground*, *Apple Tree House* and *Hey Duggee* demonstrate how unconventional family dynamics can be presented inspirationally and built into the creative process. The relationship between *Treasure Champs*' protagonists Kari and Barry is built around the values explored across the series. Working together, they explore empathy and patience, teamwork and sacrifice, forgiveness and respect. In defining what makes a "family", you'd be hard pushed not to pull in at least some of these values. Kari and Barry might not be blood relations, but they're family in plenty of ways that really matter. Their very design is based on the idea that we're all essentially the same, but uniquely different.

I'm *really* excited to be part of Three Arrows' next CBeebies project because – more so than any previous pre-school series – we're going to be directly encouraging a shared viewing experience. We'll be asking parents or carers at home to actually model the activities demonstrated within the programme with their children. But before I tell you more, I'm going to veer slightly off topic...

When my son, Frank, was coming up to 12 months old I was lucky enough to be able to take a career break and look after him. It was one of the most exciting, memorable, exhausting and nerve-shredding experiences of my life. It was amazing to watch him grow, but his needs changed so quickly, I was constantly playing catch up. I was convinced I was doing everything wrong, that every other parent had things figured out better than me. Luckily, help was at hand. My community in North Manchester, like many across the UK, offers support in the form of baby and toddler groups, some privately run and some organised by the council, charities or community initiatives.

I had reservations about getting involved with baby groups. For starters, they tended to be scheduled at specific times and our timekeeping skills were a little … loose. We considered it a success if we could hit the right day, let alone the right hour or minute. But my overriding reservation was that I'd have my worse fears confirmed, that I'd be put on the spot, interrogated and shown up as the slack, disorganised, unworthy chancer of a parent that I suspected I really was.

But, being a glutton for punishment (and following some heavy cajoling from my partner) one wet Monday morning Frank and I went along to our local church-run baby group. And you know what? Once I got over the self-consciousness of being the "only dad in the room" it was all fine. Frank got to explore a new environment, see lots of new faces and play with new toys. And, despite my worst fears, I realised every other parent was just as insecure and sleep-deprived as me (although, admittedly, by and large they were much better timekeepers). We became baby group regulars. Frank's four now, but we still regularly see the friends we made at these groups over three years ago.

So, while I'm a huge advocate for these groups and appreciate the invaluable developmental, emotional and social support they offer, I have first-hand experience of the very real anxieties that can hold parents and carers back from getting involved.

Which brings me neatly back to our new CBeebies commission, a series I couldn't be more proud to be helping bring to life. This new series – provisionally titled *The Baby Club* – will aim to recreate the experience of a real life baby group for parents and their babies watching at home.

Developed by experienced producers Chris Pilkington and Emma Hyman (who will serve as executive producers on the series), *The Baby Club* is deliberately constructed to be a dual-viewing experience. There will be songs, nursery rhymes, stories and interactive play that parents and carers at home will be actively encouraged to take part in with their babies. *The Baby Club* is "family viewing" at its most deliberate – a show that, by necessity of the format, should be watched alongside another person.

This is a bold commission, not least because it is a series aimed at the very early CBeebies audience of 0–18-month-old babies. This is very much a labour of love for all involved, not least Chris and Emma who have spent considerable time nurturing the idea and working alongside child developmental charities including The Foundation Years Trust and Peeple. Their research has highlighted just how vitally important the first 18 months are for a child's social and educational development. Their findings are echoed by BBC Learning's recent commitment to early years literacy and a review by children's charity I CAN and the Royal College of Speech and Language Therapists into children's speech, language and communication needs (SLCN). Published in March 2018, the review, titled *Bercow: Ten Years On*, reported that 1.4 million children in the UK have SLCN and found that 50% of children living in areas of social disadvantage start school with delayed language needs. The review also found a link between SLCN and mental health needs. The review's chair, Jean Gross CBE, stated "We want to make children's early communication as much a priority for the nation as obesity or dental health."

The Baby Club couldn't be more timely, and a key ambition of the series is to encourage dads, as well as mums, to engage with baby groups in their community. Despite growing numbers of stay-at-home dads, most baby and toddler groups are still – in reality, if not in design – a mum-only environment. It's important that dads and male carers feel comfortable in reaching out to the support available in their community. But this responsibility shouldn't just lie with the dads. Much more can be done by early years community groups to make dads and male carers feel welcome, and more male-led groups would certainly help address the imbalance. Men are massively underrepresented in early years education – just 2% of early years educators in the UK are male – so there's a long way to go in recognising that *every* member of the family has a role to play in a child's development. As programme makers, we have the ability, and perhaps even a responsibility, to do something about this.

With increasing time and financial pressures being heaped on parents, family time is becoming ever rarer and more precious. Time keeping aside, my baby group experience was a hugely positive one, a shared experience that I'll never forget. It would be great if *The Baby Club* could encourage and empower others to have a similar experience. ◯

SOMEONE TELL THE PUPPETS TO STOP TALKING!

WILL BRENTON

—

An entirely personal view based on too many years working with kids and puppets. Two things I swore I would never do, but did, and look where that got me.

It's OK, you can stop searching now. Somebody phone the Royal Society, write to the *New Scientist*, email Sir Tim Berners-Lee, the secret of perpetual motion has been found! All you need are three things: a puppet, a puppeteer, and a reverse scan monitor. Pop a live camera feed of the puppet into the monitor and off they go.

They won't stop. Chattering, singing, walking in and out of shot, sliding up into frame, down out of frame, smiling, squishy-face frowning (technical term, obv), practising double takes and telling gags. Such is the appeal of puppets that even the puppeteers don't want to stop watching them.

A while ago, when I was directing *Playdays* (a show with a good proportion of puppets), we would play a game in the gallery between takes. If a puppet was still in shot and visible on the reverse scan monitor, the puppeteer would chatter away without stopping. Pan the camera off and the chatter would stop. It was like a volume control. Pan on, chatter. Pan off, silence.

But we don't use puppets just to entertain ourselves. Well, most of us don't. Puppets have fascinated humans since we first picked up a woolly mammoth's tibia, drew a smiley face on the ball joint and said "Hellooo!"

I won't get too involved in the blah-blah history bit about puppets originating about 4000 years ago or the waffle-waffle part about them being inanimate objects manipulated in order to tell stories that usually reflected the society they were part of. Instead I'll fast-forward to the last few decades and talk a bit about why they are used to such great effect – and why, perhaps, they are having a little bit of a renaissance.

Which is a big word for a bit of foam on a stick.

There is an apocryphal tale about a person with a puppet sitting amongst a group of kids, making no effort to conceal the fact they are operating the puppet and doing the voice, yet being totally ignored by the kids as they all focused on the puppet. Why?

What, exactly, is the appeal?

To begin with, there is the look. The best puppet makers use colour and texture to create quirky designs which bestow incredible personality on puppets that, coupled with the skilled animation of the puppeteer, is so effective your eyes can't help but be drawn to them. Any producer of a kids' TV show should be tempted by the fact that they can make their cast so visually appealing. It's one of the first challenges of character creation accomplished – getting your audience's attention.

But I don't think that is what is at the heart of a puppet's appeal.

Perhaps it's that many puppets look like a soft toy – playing to our instinct for protecting and nurturing, our instinct to "look after" things. (*It's real – scientists are doing papers on it and everything…*) The connection can be so strong that there are many people who believe that soft toys actually have feelings. (*Oh God… Sorry, Mr Bear…*) It is easy to see this transferred onto a puppet. This instinctive reaction might accomplish another big challenge we face when creating characters, which is getting people to care.

But I don't think it's that either.

Personality is a big factor. Puppets have huge personalities which leap off screen. They have big eyes, funny faces, unusual voices and mannerisms. Puppets are larger than life friends who can make us laugh and giggle. And they can flip that – they can convey sadness, pain, self-doubt. That has to count for something?

Of course it does. In fact, everything I've listed above counts for a lot – and it is the combination of all these factors that make great puppets so powerful. With one crucial extra.

Licence.

Puppets have licence. They can do and say things that a human can't get away with. They can push the boundaries of what is acceptable, go to places that no actor, and certainly no presenter can go. Think of the classic puppet characters – Mr Punch taking on the world, Emu attacking, Basil Brush flirting, Statler and Waldorf shouting insults from the balcony, Hacker, Zig and Zag asking the unaskable, and of course the entire cast of *Spitting Image*. Puppets do the things we wish we could do and they do them with humour and charm. In what other world could a pig and a frog carry on a relationship?

And of course, it isn't just the funny stuff. Puppets can convey incredibly powerful emotions – think of *The Lion King* onstage, the experiences of Joey in *War Horse*. Then remember Kermit halfway up the stairs, Elmo beginning to understand the world, Deep, Kiwa, Riz, Jobi and Petal in *Get Well Soon* – characters who can talk about their fears more articulately and more comfortably than a real child might.

In theatre, we are in the middle of a huge renaissance of puppetry, arguably started by The *Lion King* and *War Horse* and continued with productions such as *The Grinning Man*, *The Light Princess* and *Pinocchio*. But what is it that makes puppets so effective in story-telling?

I think it is because there is something about a puppet that is safe. Puppets can heighten the humour, raise the anarchy, AND discuss difficult subjects and convey real emotion, but it is somehow less confrontational than watching a "real" person do it (or, somehow, an animated character) – and that means we don't look away. We see *more* of it, and that helps to really communicate the story or message we might want to get across. This safety is especially important for our young audience. Hearing a puppet character talk about an issue somehow creates a safe zone, without diminishing the power of the topic in any way. And that is a unique ability.

So… Puppets are not just a way of waving a brightly coloured stuffed thing in front of kids to get their attention, but rather a way of combining anarchic entertainment with honesty and empathy, opening the path for a trusting relationship between the viewer and the character. Any writer or producer should seriously consider how using the right puppet character can facilitate incredible content for their audience.

Oh. And they make great plush toys. Which helps. ◔

Puppeteer Louise Gold and the Queen visit CMC 2017. copyright: jenniferbooth.carbonmade.com

TIME FOR THE GAME CHANGERS TO CHANGE THEIR GAME

ED PETRIE

—

"Having spent 12 years working in kids' TV (first Nickelodeon and then CBBC) and seeing the thought and care that goes into providing content for young people, there needs to be some serious questions asked about how YouTube functions."

That was the tweet I rattled off on the train at the start of the new year, on my way to have custard pies thrown in my face and make fart jokes performing in panto in Sevenoaks. It was in response to a story I'd just seen about yet another YouTuber scandal, this time Logan Paul, who uploaded a video making wisecracks in front of the body of a man in Japan who had recently committed suicide. Most people would have had a strong response to that news, and on this occasion I let my thumbs get the better of me, knocking off that tweet and a few others before I reached the station. By the time I reached the theatre, the retweets and likes had got a bit out of control. I spent the next few weeks hiding behind my agent's skirts while she skilfully negotiated interviews with news organisations and radio stations as I tried to make the point that something was broken in our industry and we all needed to come together and fix it.

I'm normally a very well behaved CBBC presenter and, remembering my training back in 2007, try to keep my opinions to myself (despite being freelance these days). But like so many other industries, in children's media we've all felt the sand shifting beneath our feet while the likes of YouTube, Amazon and Snapchat ruthlessly and successfully apply their business model of minimum responsibility / maximum disruption (Facebook summed it up best, with its old mantra "move fast and break things"). They pay scant regard to the "baggage" of regulations that their competitors have adhered to for decades, and they've reaped the rewards. Individual liberty and the right of the consumer to avoid "gate keepers" controlling what they see has driven the pioneers of Silicon Valley for decades, and I'm in no position to start

mouthing off about most of that stuff – I am, as I have already made clear, a man who has custard pies splatted in his face for a living. But I do know a bit about providing entertainment for children, and I also feel most people understand that a child's freedom to do as they please is more limited than an adult's, and that us big people have great responsibility for them.

"It's the parents' responsibility!" shout the Internet libertarians, skipping off with their fingers in their ears. But my particular beef, which I have been ... er ... marinating since the start of the year, is that if you move into the marketplace of providing a platform expressly for children's content, then you have responsibilities as well. That's exactly what YouTube did with the creation of the YouTube Kids app, an app branded as child friendly because an algorithm filters out a certain amount of unsuitable content, leaving kids and parents to report any residual inappropriate content that may have slipped through.

If there's one thing that YouTube has done that betrays its lack of understanding about child protection, it's this. CBBC's *Newsround* pointed

out that this approach still exposes children to harmful content, just less of it. The response from YouTube? "We have a responsibility to make sure the platform can survive and can thrive so that we have a collection that comes from around the world on there." No, you don't. You have a responsibility to the children viewing it. That's blazingly obvious to anyone who's worked in children's entertainment, and indeed the NSPCC, whom I have spoken to in the course of all this and who have their head in their hands about it all. Unfortunately, when my MP passed on my concerns to the Department for Digital, Culture, Media and Sport, I got a letter back telling me that the Department meets with YouTube regularly, everything's great, and if I was worried about content for children, had I seen the new YouTube Kids app, which filters content to make it super safe for kids? Considering it was the very thing I was writing to them to complain about, I guess they hadn't taken much time to read my letter. And it did suggest that YouTube had done a pretty good job convincing the government not to worry about this stuff. Thankfully, recent

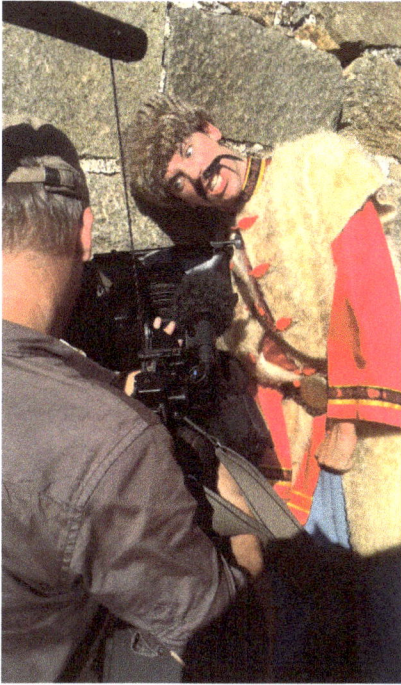

announcements from Matt Hancock, the Culture Secretary, suggest that they might finally be starting to realise that they've had the wool pulled over their eyes.

It should be stated that YouTube recently adapted their app, giving the option to switch on filters which provide content from trusted partners and channels that moderators have verified as responsible and safe. This is a start, but it's still not good enough. Why are these features only an option?! It's a kids' app, for kids. Disney films don't come with an option that allows the possibility of David Icke popping up to tell your children that lizards run the world. Nickelodeon shows don't have an option for your kids to stumble across an animation of SpongeBob SquarePants having his liver removed. YouTube just can't get its head around the fact that when you're expressly providing content for kids, there is an ethical need for an actual human being viewing it with their eyes and ears *before* it reaches a child's brain. If you're in that marketplace, that should be the baseline requirement (and no, more moderators sifting through stuff after it's been uploaded is not the answer, despite YouTube's insistence that that will do just fine). By running the app this way, YouTube still shifts the responsibility for its content to parents, and with a recent US survey finding that 22% of parents didn't even know that YouTube had safety features, that's a lot of kids who will still be exposed to content that is unsuitable.

The government is only just starting to get to grips with this issue, and YouTube, along with similar sites, are dragging their heels. So, what's to be done? I think it's up to the rest of us, who do understand our responsibilities, to put our necks on the line and risk annoying these big players by relentlessly reminding them that this isn't acceptable, and we should show the way by resisting the temptation to let our own standards slip. Good examples of the right way of doing things are SuperAwesome's curated PopJam app and the recently launched CBBC Buzz app, where 40 moderated pieces of content are uploaded every day. I think most parents would agree that in the time between coming home from school and going to bed, that's probably more than enough. And let's work with organisations like the NSPCC to try and persuade regulators that the light hand of regulation which has been fashionable for the last decade or so isn't a model that works when it comes to providing content for our children, who need our protection, help and guidance. And the occasional fart joke. ☺

TECH TO REMEMBER – ONGOING INNOVATIONS IN THE WAY KIDS INTERACT WITH MEDIA

ALEX MILNE TURNER

—

Perhaps it is Kermit the Frog who evokes pangs of nostalgia in you, or maybe it's Zebedee who takes you on a stroll down memory lane. Whether it's *The Muppet Show* or *The Magic Roundabout,* our childhood memories were inexorably shaped by one central technology – the television set.

Since the television, tablets and smartphones have had a drastic impact on the way children consume media. Due to their portability and connectivity, these household items have enabled content to be accessed by kids in their bedrooms, on a bus, or at the table in a restaurant.

However, we believe the next wave of technologies to reshape the children's media landscape will change the way audiences *interact* with content. More compelling than merely smaller screens, technologies such as augmented reality (AR), toys-to-life and voice-powered home assistants are creating new and exciting opportunities for children's media producers.

In the 2018 Children's Media Conference discussion: "Technology - What's Next" my company MTM will highlight a few recent developments in interactive technology that have caught our eye.

CAN I TOUCH IT?

AR overlays digital media and information onto the physical world. Catapulted into our collective consciousness through Niantic's *Pokémon GO,* the technology uses everyday devices, such as smartphones and tablets, to enhance the world around us.

Over the past decade, AR has had a lasting impact on medicine, the military and education, but it is now the

world of children's publishing which is experiencing this transformation most astutely. Characters and images once restricted to the page are awoken through AR as the technology "changes the way children interact with the world", as noted by Google's Luca Prasso at last month's publishing and tech conference "Dust or Magic".

US-based Carlton Books is ahead of this trend, selling over three million books powered by its proprietary AR technology platform *Digital Magic*. The books cover a variety of popular children's topics, including dinosaurs, bugs and Transformers, enlivening the characters with a supplementary mobile app; offering children a more tangible connection to their heroes.

A UK start-up, Mardles, is taking this one step further. Using similar technology, Mardles has incorporated AR into a set of stickers and a "4D colouring book". The book uses AR technology to create a virtual asset of a child's drawing, replicating their colouring choices. Online forums are expected to be the next step – where children can build their own 3D environments to consume content and socialise – and with Niantic's next AR adventure set to be *Harry Potter*, we think augmented mania is only just beginning.

IT'S ALIVE!

Another area where new forms of interaction are being forged is digitally connected toys, or toys-to-life. Toys-to-life is not a new phenomenon, and there are already classic properties such as *LEGO Dimensions* and *Skylanders* – the latter accruing billions of dollars in hardware sales. Despite these successes though, many industry commentators are sceptical about the future of this category of licensed product.

However, the market is producing exciting innovations in the space. For example, Microsoft researchers have developed a prototype smart playmat called Project Zanzibar, a cutting-edge consumer sensor that can locate and scan objects to be turned into digital assets.

Project Zanzibar enables kids to play with toys, cards and blocks as their actions come alive onscreen. Children can even introduce their own playthings, such as personal dolls, to sessions, manipulating them with their hand movements mirrored on a digital platform.

Developments such as these deliver a more tactile, agile learning and engagement environment. From drawing imaginary shapes to lighting a movie set featuring a favoured teddy bear, toys-to-life provides a universe to populate with ideas and fill with playthings.

OH, HEY THERE BERT!

Voice and home assistants are already reshaping the way young audiences interact with media and entertainment. Amazon's voice assistant Alexa, the market leader via Amazon's Echo devices, has launched a set of skills-based games aimed at children, with Nickelodeon's SpongeBob and Sesame Street's Elmo first entering the scene.

In Nickelodeon's *The SpongeBob Challenge*, kids become a new Krusty Krab restaurant employee tasked with taking increasingly complicated food orders, before relaying those orders to SpongeBob, Squidward and Mr. Krabs. In Sesame Street's application, meanwhile, kids practise their alphabet by playing hide and seek with Elmo, using audio clues to find out where he might be.

There are clear benefits for interaction and engagement with kids' content, but it is also important for producers and broadcasters to bear in mind the unique position these devices enjoy. As they give access to more kids' content from more providers, Alexa and Google Assistant are fundamentally changing the way in which children will discover new content in the future.

As children look back on their childhood, it is certain to be shaped by more than just the television. Multiple platforms across many devices will mould children's earliest memories, providing opportunities to interact in new and exciting ways.

"DOING MORE" TO KEEP CHILDREN "SAFE" ONLINE?

ANDY PHIPPEN

—

In recent times, it seems that rarely a week goes by without a senior policy figure calling for the technology and media industry to "do more" to ensure children and young people can be safe online.

In the last year, we have seen calls for platform and content providers to ensure children can't see "sexualised imagery", pornography, material of a terrorist nature, abuse from peers, "self-generated" indecent content, and to ensure their screen time is controlled. Platform and content providers, we are told, are the ones who provide access to this material and therefore should ensure that it is only seen by those who are mature enough to take a critical perspective and will not be harmed by what they see

However, while these media soundbites might be easy to throw out, how much can a platform or content provider actually do to ensure children are "safe" from the perils of the online world and the content it provides? We now have reporting routes, take-downs, warnings around content, algorithms which attempt to identify specific types of content through keyword matching, pre-screening of some content and means to block abusers. Yet providers are still told to "do more" – to be moral guardians as well as providers, to be proactive in ensuring every child is free from abuse and harm when going online.

However, even with a little unpicking we see how ridiculous some of these calls are. For example, social media providers were recently told to monitor the screen time of young users of their sites to ensure they can only be online for a limited amount of time per day. But how could this work in practice? While we have the mantra "no under 13s on social media" (even though most incorrectly claim this is for safeguarding reasons, rather than an arbitrary value defined in US law related to parental consent around advertising), it is actually very difficult for a 13-year-old to prove their age in a consistent and uniform manner across a whole population. And even if we get to a position where this is no longer the case, how can social media providers, as a collective, determine how long a young person has spent online in a specific day, given that their screen time is likely to be spread across multiple platforms? Surely this would require data sharing between organisations, which would seriously impact upon the child's right to privacy and the data protection responsibilities of the providers?

Taking another example, at the end of 2016 the Secretary of State for Health called on mobile phone providers to install "an algorithm" on a child's phone to determine if the image they have just taken is indecent. How might an algorithm determine if something is indecent? While we have clear legal definitions for obscenity, indecency is a far more complex and subjective concept. Are we really expecting service providers to implement algorithms determining the decency of an image when we have no formal definition of what this is? Perhaps the algorithm should be trained using images

similar to the ones being detected – in this case indecent images of children? And even if such an algorithm did exist, would we be happy with service providers scanning the phones of minors to determine the decency of the images they take and controlling their right to expression? While the non-consensual sharing of indecent images is a problem for both the youth and adult population, algorithms do not provide the solution.

At best, this is naïve policy making intended to maximise media coverage, done without much thought for the practical implications of what is called for. Policy makers need to realise that Ranum's Law[1] is in effect – "you don't solve social problems with software".

This knee-jerk policy approach has existed for a quite a while and has been identified in geek culture. The "Four Horsemen of the Infopocalypse" is a term coined by Timothy C May in 1988[2] to reflect the typical policy response to any technological innovation a government might wish to control. To win over public opinion to back tougher regulation, a government can claim the tech is used by one or more of the Four Horsemen: terrorists, paedophiles, drug dealers, and money launderers. While May introduced this concept related to controlling the use of encryption by the public (and we can still see the ripples of this to this day, with Amber Rudd's claim that "ordinary people" don't need to use encryption in 2017, for

1 http://seclists.org/firewall-wizards/1999/Jun/186

2 http://www.firstmonday.org/ojs/index.php/fm/article/view/1999/1874

example), we can see this applied to many technological innovations, such as Tor, Whatsapp, Bitcoin, peer-to-peer file sharing and social media in general. The general approach is similar every time:

1. Identify a target that you wish to control or legislate.
2. Identify a common fear most people have that is difficult to defend against, such as one of the Four Horsemen of the Infopocalypse.
3. Use the media to show that the target is used by these groups (while ignoring many more prevalent positive uses of the target).
4. Claim that banning or controlling the target is the only way to prevent the bad guys using it, and if you're opposed to that, the bad guys win.

The current age verification debacle can be seen to emerge from this very approach. There have been calls for providers to "do more" to ensure children cannot access pornography from 2012. This has led to the filtering of public Wi-Fi (to prevent the viewing and "use" of pornography in cafes and similar, an apocryphal phenomenon if ever there was one) and all major ISPs now provide "family friendly" filters for parents to install at home (although the number who choose to do so does not seem very high). More recently a Conservative Party Manifesto commitment promised that:

"We will stop children's exposure to harmful sexualised content online, by requiring age verification for access to all sites containing pornographic material and age-rating for all music videos."

This commitment resulted in the legislation that now makes up section 14–30 of the Digital Economy Act 2017, which empowers the BBFC to police age verification of all commercial pornography providers with access in the UK. However, how this age verification is done was never defined or even explored prior to the requirement becoming law and we now have proposals such as pornography companies providing age verification solutions themselves (which has already been identified as a serious conflict of interest and potentially massive privacy risk), proof of age using passport and driving licence data, or popping into the local newsagent to buy a "porn pass" which will provide the purchaser with the means to access legal content using a unique identifier that allows them to anonymous and uniquely verify that they are an adult.

In order to keep children safe, it seems, we must impose greater restrictions on the adult population as well as eroding the rights of children themselves. We have a creeping agenda of increased control over the content children can see (most of us working in this field are very aware that filtering sexually explicit content will also restrict access to valuable resources such as information related to sexuality, gender, STIs, etc.), monitoring access at school and at home and even tracking children on their devices, in order to reassure ourselves that they are safe, free from harm and protected from any content that might upset them. And if you oppose this position, clearly you don't want children to be safe. If you do not support age verification and filtering, you must want children to see pornography. Do you want children to see pornography?

Perhaps a more pragmatic perspective would be "children are accessing pornography and will continue to do so regardless of the technical blocks we try to put in place, so we should look at education policy that might help with critical thinking around sexually explicit materials and their influence". However, this is less likely to result in positive media headlines.

In our race to make children safe, we have lost sight of a fundamental issue raised with me by a 10-year-old boy during a school visit – "What do we mean by safe anyway?". Safety with a prohibitive flavour always comes with caveats. What happens when one of our safety barriers fails? What happens if the barriers don't address a new threat? What if there is such a broad range of issues which can result in distress for children online, that preventing them from ever being exposed to said issues is a pipe dream?

Clearly technology can be a useful tool, and I see providers doing a great deal to make use of technology in ways that are reasonable to implement, such as reporting routes, blocking, etc. However, technology will only go so far.

Personally, I would rather have resilient children than safe ones. Yet it would seem that in our rush to keep children safe, we are not considering that resilience comes from exposure to risk, rather than being hidden from it. But that risk should be addressed in safe spaces and in measured ways – through the development of critical thinking in education, developing key themes and

understanding from an early age, gaining knowledge around issues of consent, boundaries, privacy and respect. While providers certainly do have a responsibility toward the wellbeing of children who engage with their sites, this is not an exclusive responsibility. A parent would not expect a playground provider to hold all of the solutions to playing on their equipment in a park. Yes, we would expect them to ensure the environment was safe and in good working order, but we would also expect parents to remain with the child and play a role in keeping them safe, and we would expect the child to understand how to use the play equipment safely. Why should this be different in the online world? Providers need to understand their responsibility and act upon them, but so do policy makers, professionals, parents and others with safeguarding duties around children and young people. When some stakeholders are doing little more than pointing the fingers at others, saying "you, do more!", we will never effectively develop online resilience among our young people. Technology will not solve this, education will. ◯

IF TEENAGERS TAUGHT ONLINE SAFETY...

ESTELLE LLOYD

—

"Perspectives of young people should be at the forefront of conversations about resilience online."

This quote from last year's Yearbook struck a chord. At Azoomee, like all ethical children's media companies, we have an integral commitment to children's safety, and as the first generation of digital natives reaches adolescence, we have an opportunity to understand the impact of their experiences.

Teenagers have experienced the digital world in a way adults cannot comparatively understand, and so, in the summer of 2017, we surveyed 300 teenagers with questions concerning their online experiences; how they dealt with them and their opinions on how the online environment affects children and young people today. 58% of respondents were female, 41% male and 1% defined themselves as other or preferred not to disclose their gender. Below are the main observations drawn from the survey and follow-up interviews with some of the participants.

ON NEGATIVE EXPERIENCES

When asked if they had encountered any negative experiences online between the ages of 7–12 years, 86% of respondents said yes. From a 14-year-old boy who saw porn aged 8 and continued to watch it despite it having "messed him up", to an 18-year-old girl who'd shared naked pictures of herself believing that the people who saw them cared about her:

> "I saw porn when I was like 8 and it messed me up. Thing is I started watching it a lot after that. I was too young."
> – male, 14

"I did end up sharing pictures of myself... I guess it made me feel grown-up and that someone cared about me. I didn't realise that they didn't care about me ... they just wanted me to show them naked pictures."
– female, 18

ON RESILIENCE

And what of the effect this is having upon our generation of guinea pig digital natives? Only 19% of the teenagers we spoke to claimed that the negative experiences they had when they were younger have had a lasting effect:

"Honestly people should find it easier to just ignore comments and dumb stuff that people say – they're just letters and it's so not worth getting worked up about it."
– male, 16

"I didn't get too upset about it because I have so many other things going on in my life, like I don't have time to worry and think about what someone thinks of me."
– female, 17

"I needed to speak to someone to get my thoughts together... I went online again but this time I spoke to someone through Relate. It really helped me."
– female, 15

ON E-SAFETY EDUCATION

Far more children are turning to peers for advice and support and we saw two main reasons for this. It's tempting for the current generation of teachers and caregivers to compare their own screen-free childhoods positively and nostalgically against today's digital childhoods. The message this sends is that we don't understand, that we are out of touch and feel ill at ease with something so integral to the lives of today's children. Asked about e-safety education taught by teachers, these teenagers' quotes reflect the general sentiment of the respondents:

"They'll always talk about it in a negative way like, 'That's not my generation, I would have never done this as a kid'. The fact of the matter is it's still their children who are. If parents learned about it themselves, they'd be more understanding. That's how I am with my little sister. I do actually get where she is coming from where my parents maybe would not."
– female, 18

"In my first year, we had a sort of brief technology meeting and whilst there were good intentions, the principal was saying things that were like completely mundane and normal for us. We just thought of him as being someone who was just an old geezer who didn't know what technology was."
– female, 17

"I just feel like parents don't really understand the pressures and children's desire to be online. They'll always talk about it in a negative way but if parents learned it themselves they'd be more understanding."
– female, 18

Some teenagers referred to examples of teachers sharing news stories involving online grooming of local children, despite the interviewees living more than 200 miles apart. Of course, these cases are horrifying, and true, but they are also rare, which makes it easy for young people to dismiss them as irrelevant:

"You can be safer if you know what to do. I think sometimes when they [schools] use the examples of these horrible things, it's very rare. It happens, but it's very rare and I think if they talked about being online in terms of mental health or privacy settings or things that people actually experience then it would have a bigger impact."
– female, 19

ON THE IMPACT OF SOCIAL MEDIA

When we spoke to teens about their concerns for younger children, social media came up repeatedly, from peer pressure or online bullying, to concerns about location services, privacy, fake news and the pressure to have a follow-worthy profile. Whilst the majority (83%) felt that social media was not safe for primary-aged children to use, they agreed it will continue to be used regardless and therefore children needed to be taught how to use it smartly and safely:

"I was bullied online and then I decided to cyberbully people too because it happened to me. I trolled people and made lots of fake accounts to do it. I still feel really embarrassed I did that. I feel shame

that I could do it when I knew how bad it would be hurting because I was hurting when people did it to me."
– male, 18

"I think you have to talk to children about social media too because they will know about it. It would be hard not to know about it."
– male, 14

Our interviewees spoke about the standards of perfection they felt held to online having a profound effect on their mental health. Even equipped with the understanding that profiles on platforms like Instagram show only a snippet of someone's life, teenagers still felt the pressure to produce similar profiles themselves. Some of their responses highlight the struggle between wanting to be critical about this issue and yet conforming to it:

"I think that starts very young. At first you try to recreate it, but like you can't do it at the same level because you're not experienced ... you think, 'oh there's just something wrong with me'. I'm still kind of working on it, but I work a lot to be aware that like these are hyper-edited, very small portions of people's lives."
– female, 17

On speaking about the pressure that her 10-year-old sister and her friends face to post regularly and be validated, one 17-year-old said:

"Her friends accept absolutely anyone just so that they look like

they have a lot of followers ... that
is quite an important factor, just like
getting a lot of likes on a picture."
–female, 17

remaining mindful and vigilant of the challenges it also presents. Let's all listen, and let's respond. ◯

ON POSITIVE SCREEN TIME

All of the teenagers we interviewed were using the internet to create content linked to their interests. From shooting and editing YouTube videos, coding games, setting up a teen feminist group, even promoting their own business; teenagers are harnessing the internet's potential to work for them:

"I got really into women's rights and feminism... I think that being able to go on Instagram and see all these people who share the same views as me, it was very empowering."
– female, 17

The online world can be a source of inspiration, as well as a place for positive feedback:

"I feel like if I hadn't seen other people doing stuff like that online I never would have been inspired to write. When you get all these lovely comments and like, positive feedback it gives you a confidence boost."
– female, 18

Providing children with the information and support they need to navigate the risks of the online world will build their self-confidence and foster a responsible generation. A generation which proudly celebrates the enormous positives to come from the Internet, such as diversity, inclusion, creativity and opportunity, whilst

FINDING YOUR VOICE

ANNA CAMPBELL

———

Voice technology is shaping up to revolutionise the way children engage with media. So how does voice fit into family life, and what does it mean for brands?

The rapid take-up of voice technology in the home has caught many by surprise. For children, voice is already changing their digital lives, and providing new opportunities to discover, learn, play and communicate. But to really understand the impact of voice technology, it is important to understand how it is being used in the home, and how it is taking its place in day-to-day family life.

So what impact is voice already having on the family dynamic? What will it have to deliver to better meet the needs of all the family in the future? What are the early concerns around the new technology?

And what does it mean for brands looking to engage children and build loyal relationships?

At Sparkler, we've spent time with families who are using a wide range of voice platforms, from remote controls, tablets and phones, to voice assistants across the home. We have found that children are using voice for a wide range of activities throughout the day; from jokes to homework help, random searches for all kinds of information, searching for clips, music and programmes.

Most strikingly, we have found that children are engaging with voice in a very different way to adults. Unlike adults, children don't have to learn or unlearn anything. They're straight off the blocks as soon as they can speak. Children don't wait to be told what they can use voice for; they explore and discover as they go.

Children also use more conversational language. Adults tend to struggle more with being informal and conversational; we have to unlearn our text search rules, our formal ways of interacting, and we can often feel uncomfortable barking commands. In contrast, children can have a more empathetic relationship with Voice. In fact, a recent MIT study found that children perceive their voice provider to be friendly and trustworthy – and often consider them a friend.

What this means is that children are naturally overcoming some of the usage and discovery barriers that can stand in the way for adults, and are instinctively exploring the possibilities that Voice offers. They're used to learning through play, and picking up tips and tricks as they try things out. They are naturally investigative, and build knowledge incrementally as they go. Ultimately, children want voice tech to "learn them". They want it to get to know them and to deliver more experiences "it knows" they will like.

In the case of TV programmes, voice is changing not only what children watch, but how they watch. Children are using voice remote controls before they can use traditional remotes. They have control over the content they're watching on the TV earlier. Using voice search on tablets and phones is also affecting how kids find and watch TV programmes and related content.

All this looks likely to impact on children's relationship with characters, programmes and channels.

For older children, using voice is changing the way they navigate TV content – from initial discovery through to loyalty to particular programmes, and what to watch next.

To drive discovery, channels and programme makers need to understand how children use voice, and use those insights to meet them where they already are. Kids' established discovery channels are helping kids find out about new things they can do with voice. YouTubers are showing off the possibilities of the tech and suggesting new tips and skills.

So, what is the broader impact of voice on families and household dynamics? Some concerns have already arisen. Whereas access for all can be seen as democratising, some parents worry that the use of voice in the home may interrupt the flow of family conversation. More significantly, some parents are concerned about their young children's uncontrolled access to information. The tech is not yet sophisticated enough to cater for different ages and development stages. For example, different assistants can give very different answers to the question of where babies come from…

And what will be the long-term impact of voice on children's behaviour? Some children brought up with voice have been shown to be less adept at understanding facial expressions. Some are concerned about the impact on manners as kids become used to barking commands!

However, for companies and creatives, voice presents new opportunities to reach children, with the potential to build closer, more loyal relationships with brands.

In a voice environment, there needs to be careful consideration of what it means for the brand relationship. Crucially, kids engage with characters, so careful thought needs to be given to each brand's "character", and how best to drive brand attribution. What personality, gender, accent is most engaging and fits best?

At the same time, brand loyalty among parents may be undermined with voice. To date, parents have been the primary gatekeepers of younger children's content. When children use voice, their choices are not mediated by parents – they go directly to their own choice of content.

Ultimately, voice needs to fulfil different roles for different family members at different times, with the character and personality to suit, anticipating family needs and adapting to occasions. Voice needs to meet different needs throughout the day – whether it be homework help, a PA in the morning, a life coach, and ultimately a trustworthy source of learning, fun and enrichment.

The enthusiasm for voice is evident from the speed of adoption and the intuitive ways that children are using the new technology. The big challenge now is to understand how children can have a richer, more intuitive relationship with voice, and to help them make the most of the new opportunities to discover, play and learn.

○

ALEXA, WHAT'S THE FUTURE OF VOICE RECOGNITION FOR KIDS?

GARY POPE

—

Smart speakers are appearing in more and more homes. Currently, one in six Americans now own a smart speaker, up 128% from January 2017. With half of all our searches expected to be performed using voice by 2020, voice recognition is set to become a part of everyday life. And children are at the heart of this trend. Parents are recognising the value of voice recognition technology for children, with 57% of smart speakers bought to entertain children, and 88% saying that their children enjoyed Amazon's smart assistant, Alexa. Even though the touch screen era is still in its fairly early stages, parents are already concerned about the amount of screen time their children are exposed to. Could voice recognition be the user interface antidote?

The surge of interest in smart speakers is primarily fuelled by two things – devices are getting cheaper and the voice recognition technology being used has vastly improved. Previous iterations had glitches, along with difficulties picking up accents and children's voices. It takes huge computing power and innovation to break down human speech in real time and before now, the end product was just not advanced enough. Now we have superior machine learning and AI that can make conversations with a device truly possible. Just look at the way Google booked a hairdressing appointment at the Google Developers' Conference ... if that's what they're showing us, can you imagine what's under the counter?

Smart speakers have the potential to become an integral part of everyday home life. A quite wonderfully bizarre statistic is that in a study we undertook, 22% of parents said that their virtual assistant was like another part of the family. I pity their children. And of respondents who use virtual assistants, 42% said they spoke to them as if they were real people, with a similar number assigning their virtual assistant a gender. This acceptance of virtual assistants is of course utterly in keeping with the fearless relationship with technology that children

enjoy. In 2012, the University of Washington studied 90 children interacting with a life-size robot called Robovie and found that children thought Robovie had "mental states" and was a "social being". When he was put in a closet, more than half of the children thought this wasn't fair. A similar emotional connection is taking hold with Alexa and

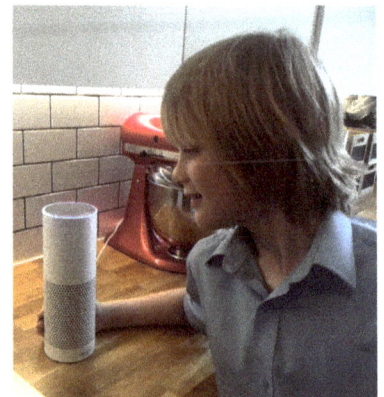

other assistants. But then, I remember being quite upset for my speaking Yoda toy when he was locked in the cupboard by an irritated colleague.

Earlier this year we undertook a study to get to grips with the reality of smart speakers – how do children actually interact with them? Not unsurprisingly, usage differs between age groups. Younger children will try to get to know this new digital pal by asking lots of questions like, "What's your favourite food?" and "Do you have any other friends?". In most interactions younger children also got very close to the device. In comparison, older children were more interested in testing it, asking questions like "What are you?" and "Who is the lead character in LEGO Ninjago?". This is broadly in keeping with their social and cognitive development stage.

Interacting with voice recognition devices clearly has a huge part to play in helping develop a child's language skills. Children were quick to learn that they needed to be quiet when someone else was talking to the smart speaker. This is an important skill that children are open to learning around the age of four or five, and a far cry from the scare a few months ago that

all children would be rude from now on because you didn't need to say "please" to get Alexa to do something.

Particular uses specific to children and our industry are of course story-telling and gaming. Alexa can be used to read stories to children when parents are unable to, plugging a gap that might otherwise be filled with more mindless time on a tablet. In this regard, smart speakers are not a substitute for human interaction, but something that is supplementary.

During our study, younger children in the pre-operational stage particularly enjoyed story and learning-led apps – just as they would on a screen-led device. Children need to be able to follow along easily to enjoy something by themselves, benefiting from simple commands, a strong feedback loop, predictability and the ability to dip in and out quickly – good software on a good digital assistant does this. All the parents we spoke with tended to feel more comfortable with this type of entertainment compared to what can be seen as mindless computer screen time. For older children (6–8-year-olds) whose emerging autonomy means they need a little more control over things, customisation is more

interesting, something that is currently not an important feature of smart speakers. To appeal to this age group, continuity and empowerment are fundamentally important. Memory, social, narrative and competitive games are all possibilities for this group.

However, there needs to be balance between when a child uses a smart speaker and when they use their own creativity and initiative. For example, the new Echo Dot for kids can be programmed so that it always responds to a child saying, "I'm bored" with some stimulation. While this is smart, it doesn't allow for the fact that boredom breeds possibilities. It's fundamentally important for children to decide independently whether they should play a game, play outside or go and do something less boring instead under their own steam.

The challenge for the smart speaker space lies in being able to infuse the magic of an engaging entertainment experience without the use of a visual aid. The software has to be good and whilst it's coming along, it's not quite there yet. But then, just like the tablet in 2010, this device wasn't designed for children … it was adopted by children and then design followed. ○

NO SNOWFLAKES PLEASE, WE'RE GRANGE HILL

DIANA HINSHELWOOD

—

Kids today, eh? What are they like? No respect. In my day, we didn't … etc. etc. Despite obvious differences in technology and taste in music, kids are more similar to us when we were at school than we think.

Getting your own back on teachers, making excuses for not doing your homework, trying to make your school uniform look cool. Sound familiar?

How about student/ teacher affairs, bullying, drug addiction? We may not have experienced them personally, but we were aware they went on. And they still feature in our newsfeeds today.

Up until the late '70s, school life in drama was portrayed as a glorious Enid Blyton type jape, all washed down with lashings of ginger beer. At best, it was St Trinian's. At worst, it was Billy Bunter.

And then, on 8 February 1978, Children's BBC unleased *Grange Hill* on to TV screens and into the lives of school children all over the land. Controversial from the start, its gritty mix of issues and messy friendships gave school children a voice of their own and reflected their real lives rather than the idealised versions we'd seen before. It cut across class – whether you went to Eton or the local comprehensive, the shared experience of school life was instantly recognisable. Children loved it. Grown-ups hated it – which was of course an even bigger reason for children to love it!

The Establishment were instantly outraged at the depiction of unruly pupils, but despite their antipathy, the Home Office gradually came to see *Grange Hill* as a useful tool for campaigning and highlighting issues, such as the powerful story of Zammo's drug addiction and the "Just Say No" campaign that accompanied it. There may have been anarchy in the classroom, but *Grange Hill* was deeply moral. Everyone got their come-uppance, though not in the judgemental, do-goody way of today. However, the BBC hierarchy remained implacable in their dislike. I was once told by someone very senior that children's telly wasn't real telly – which probably explains their alarm. *Grange Hill* was very real.

Its creator, Phil Redmond, had pitched the idea to broadcasters with no luck until Anna Home at BBC Children's decided to take a risk.

Originally commissioned as a one-off series, *Grange Hill* ran for an incredible 30 years, first on BBC1 and then on the CBBC channel. The programme had an immediate impact. It was controversial and realistic from the beginning, mixing comedy with adventures. It created unforgettable characters such as Tucker Jenkins, Zammo, Gonch and Hollo who were much loved and are remembered today with great affection. This was demonstrated by the huge success of the recent 40-year-anniversary seminar at Royal Holloway University, where middle-aged fans came armed with cameras and autograph

books. However, by the end of its run, the series had lost its rough edge of authenticity, so much so that Phil Redmond commented it was no longer the show it was intended to be.

At the time *Grange Hill* was commissioned, BBC Children's audience included secondary school children and reached into mid-teens, so it was easier to tackle tough storylines. However, the digital media revolution changed not only production techniques but viewing habits too. The BBC found itself losing its young teen audience to new channels dedicated to youth programming. YouTube and streaming gave teens more choice in how and when they watched. It was generally felt that there wasn't much point in trying to keep them, so the age of the target audience for *Grange Hill* was lowered to under 12, and finally to nine. Inevitably, the themes had to reflect that, and as the audience grew younger, the controversial issues were dropped and storylines were softened.

Social media had an effect too. It created a platform to voice opinions freely, for the good and the bad. While it is good to have a say, this also allows self-styled critics to

impose their particular views on others and hound those whose opinions differ. The result is a society scared to take risks and cause offence – not a great climate for pushing boundaries.

Health and safety was also a worry, and depictions of pupils overturning tables and carrying weapons played on fears of copycat behaviour. Ironically, these modern concerns are the same as those held by the Establishment and BBC hierarchy at the start of *Grange Hill*, but today's risk-averse culture has created a nervousness about being held responsible for it.

All TV programmes have a shelf-life, so it would seem only natural that *Grange Hill* should run its course and be replaced by something considered more "relevant". Only it hasn't. Currently, there is a lack of content for 12–14-year-olds as broadcasters pulled back from creating it, arguing that this age group isn't watching any more. Despite commitments to the 10–14-year-old audience, Channel 4 now claims that teens are catered for through its family programmes. To its credit, ITV have introduced teen-led storylines to *Coronation Street* featuring drug taking and truancy and portraying teenage life in all its messy misery. All to predictable outrage.

But that is missing the point. *Grange Hill* excluded adults and gave teenagers something of their own. In the 10 years since its demise, nothing new has come close to reflecting the real lives of our school children. Because of the digital and social changes over the last 10 to 15 years, there is an opinion that a programme like *Grange Hill* wouldn't be made today. If so, that's a great shame as the issues of bullying, peer pressure and rebellion are as prevalent as ever. School kids need relatable heroes and anti-heroes, and in our era of social media where nothing is as it seems, you could argue that there is a need for some gritty realism to challenge the new caution and risk aversion.

CBBC is now widening its remit to entice the teen audience back again. To do so, it must hold its nerve against nay-sayers and offence takers. Should *Grange Hill* or another realistic school drama be made today, kids would love it. Grown-ups would hate it – but isn't that the way it should be?

PADDINGTON BEAR – AN ENDURING ICON IN OUR THROWAWAY AGE

DIANA HINSHELWOOD

—

Paddington 2 was the fourth most successful British film of 2017. Considering that this gentle, unassuming character first made his way into our hearts in 1958, that is an astonishing achievement.

In October this year, Paddington will be 60 years old. He's wearing well for a seasoned traveller and has shown us all that the key to staying young at heart is curiosity and adventure. Mind you, Paddington has some natural advantages. His fur is always insta-ready and needs no filters. His hat, coat and boots are design classics that no influencer could possibly improve. He brings his timeless adventures to a new audience in a way that YouTube vloggers can only dream about. Avocado on toast can't match the sugar rush of a marmalade sandwich, so eat your heart out, food bloggers. And no self-styled YouTube adventurer can stage a daring escape from prison as Paddington does in his latest film.

So, what is the reason that Paddington has found his way into the hearts of several generations – and stayed there? One answer, of course, is story-telling. No matter what the medium, you need content, and in our era of style over substance it is always a good story that will capture imagination. This is no surprise to us working in children's media. Children have always been the most critical of audiences, and will turn away if their attention isn't grabbed immediately. We know how to get their attention and keep it. Having said that, as times change, few children's characters have endured in the way Paddington has, and many characters from my own

childhood memories are not interesting enough to my son and his friends, which is very disappointing.

For adults, Paddington is a nostalgic treasure from childhood. For today's children, he is a funny character who makes them laugh when his good-natured efforts help lead to mayhem. Despite today's faster pace and constant visual stimulation, the classic mix of slapstick comedy and jeopardy remains appealing from generation to generation. Childlike and full of curiosity, Paddington represents the child in all of us.

But it isn't just Paddington's naïve curiosity that the young audience identify with. We also identify with the Browns, and particularly the Brown children. As a young child, who didn't want to have a wild animal living with them? Paddington is a spectacled bear from deepest Peru and he might be more mild than wild, but he beats a cat or a dog any day. Can you imagine the envy of your school friends?

And adventurers always have our respect. In 1958, international travel was not as easy as it is today, so it's incredible that Paddington managed to travel to London all by himself from so far away. It shows courage and determination – essential qualities for a hero.

Michael Bond says he based Paddington's famous suitcase and "Please look after this bear" label on his memories of children at London stations in the '40s, uprooted and sent to live with strangers in the countryside, which may as well have been a foreign country to the evacuees. Today's children may be familiar with travel, but there is drama in being separated from everyone you know, with hints of danger and the thrill of the unexpected. That is as true for stories today as it was then. What will happen? We want to know.

The story of how Paddington came about is almost as amazing as his escapades. Michael Bond was a BBC cameraman, and when he came across a lone teddy bear on a shelf in a London shop, he bought it as a Christmas present for his wife. This last minute impulse buy was the start of an incredible story that spawned many books, three animated TV series and two major films. Michael had worked on *Blue Peter*, and Paddington became involved with the programme, resulting in many appearances, further books and stories of Paddington at the BBC, including a guest appearance in the 2009 Children in Need video. Of course, his association with the national broadcaster helped to keep his profile high during the years before social media, but as the digital revolution brought a constant stream of new and relevant characters, Paddington continued to hold his place in our hearts.

Here we must mention the toy bears that are now collectors' items. I have one – now much loved by my son, and another clue to Paddington's endurance. The popularity of the Paddington Bear toy keeps the character alive, but is also an indicator of how important merchandise and branding would become for future broadcasters, TV producers and film makers. The original bear was created and manufactured in 1972 by a company famously run by Jeremy Clarkson's parents, and wasn't linked to a broadcaster or publisher, but licensed by Michael himself. The success of the bears became an obvious business model for marketing, publicity and of course generating profit. Broadcasters eventually saw the potential and now no major production deal for children's media is complete without a merchandising plan.

As we insist that content is key, we can't ignore the fact that today's young audiences expect a greater level of sophistication, and Paddington's journey through the generations has been accompanied by advances in animation and production techniques. Bizarrely, the very first Paddington TV series in 1975, produced by London based animation company, FilmFair, was the most experimental, with a stop-motion puppet in a 3D space against 2D black and white backgrounds. All the other characters were 2D drawings. This gave the series a distinctive appearance and was unusual for the mixing of techniques. The subsequent two series, in 1989

and 1997, were traditional 2D colour animations.

Following on from his success in books and TV, Paddington has now become a film star. The films, with their contemporary mix of 3D animation and live action, have given Paddington a modern, new look while still hinting at the '50s nostalgia of ordinary families living in large London houses complete with housekeeper.

Nostalgia aside, Paddington has moved with the times, making full use of digital techniques to stay relevant. He is a multimedia star across books, TV and film, with potential for further media domination in radio – particularly now Ben Whishaw has given him an instantly recognisable voice. Don't underestimate the popularity of podcasts, as technology has enabled parents to download content for later, especially useful for long car journeys.

So, Paddington's longevity owes much to adapting and being accessible to newer audiences. This is combined with a grown up's nostalgia – Paddington has essentially remained the same while other popular characters, having been given reboots, are unrecognisable from their

originals. He is a modern multimedia, cross-platform star with commercial clout, but above all it is the classic story-telling of his adventuress that keeps us coming back for more as we eagerly await Paddington 3.

Not bad for a 60-year-old. Happy Birthday, Paddington.

BLUE PETER'S BIG BIRTHDAY

EWAN VINNICOMBE

In 1958, a programme that has entertained and educated a nation and captured the hearts of millions first aired on the BBC. On Tuesday 16 October 2018, that programme, *Blue Peter*, will be celebrating its 60th birthday. *Blue Peter* holds the Guinness World Record for the longest running children's TV programme and its mission is to inspire viewers towards voyages of adventure. I'm lucky enough to be the editor of *Blue Peter* – there have been only seven in its history including the legendary Biddy Baxter and Lewis Bronze, both of whom shaped my childhood as I watched *Blue Peter* live after school. The other day it

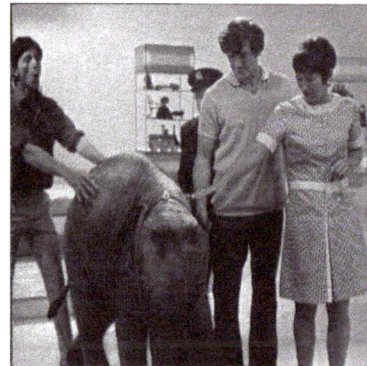

suddenly dawned on me that I started with the BBC 20 years ago. It was *Blue Peter*'s 40th birthday year and I was working on a behind-the-scenes highlights programme, *Re-Peter*. In 2008, I was the live studio producer for the 50th and now I'm editor on the 60th – I seem to enjoy a birthday!

I love *Blue Peter* to its core. It's a beast of a production to head up, demanding of your creativity, time and headspace (quite rightly so, the audience should expect and get the best), but when the content sparks the imagination of the audience and makes them join the best and biggest "badge" club in the UK, it makes it all worthwhile

Planning *Blue Peter*'s Big Birthday with the balance of past, present and future is quite an art. The famous galleon logo, created by artist Tony Hart, evokes special memories for many people who grew up watching the programme. There's the classic "here's one I made earlier", all the beloved presenters and pets, the *Blue Peter* Garden, the infamous Tracy Island craft creation, Lulu the elephant, bring and buy sales for their many successful appeals and, of course, the iconic *Blue Peter* badge. But which of those do we feature? In the end we decided on them all, with every month a focus on a particular treat for our audience.

It started on our 59th birthday with Mary Berry launching our Gold badge walk in the *Blue Peter* garden at MediaCity, then the following week Dame Jacqueline Wilson

becoming the first ever guest editor, a great start for October. With a nod to the *Blue Peter* appeals of old, Children in Need hosted a Strictly special with past presenters and then Radzi joined the RAF Falcons for an epic free fall challenge, following in the footsteps of his BP heroes John Noakes, Janet Ellis and Simon Thomas. The Duke and Duchess of Cambridge made a royal visit to our studio in December for our Christmas special and we started the new year being named the "greatest children's TV show ever" by the *Radio Times*.

On Thursday 1 February, we celebrated our 5000th programme by launching our Diamond badge, designed by international fashion designer Henry Holland. Children already need to have at least one *Blue Peter* badge and are asked to complete a series of tasks to earn the Diamond badge. Tens of thousands have already applied and the badge will only be available within our 60th year – our audience love a deadline!

In March, our annual Book Awards handed the Best Story crown to author extraordinaire,

Cressida Cowell, who made it over the Pennines (through the Beast from the East) to our studio within minutes of going live – Cressida showed a lot of BP spirit that day! And we got our trainers on for our "Mega-Mile-A-Thon" for Sport Relief with over 80 million steps pledged, showing that taking part in something big and thinking of others is still so important for *Blue Peter* viewers.

The star of the show in April was our Big Birthday Balloon created especially for our 60th year. We took a chance and decided to inflate this hot air balloon on a very

cold, blustery day on the piazza outside our studios at MediaCityUK, and the gamble paid off. Our competition winner who designed it loved seeing her creation come to life and it will feature in our 60th birthday show in a very special challenge – you can't have a birthday party without a balloon, can you?

In May, another once in a lifetime *Blue Peter* experience for Lindsey Russell was put in her diary – to fly with the Red Arrows and help launch another fantastic competition for the audience to design a Red Arrows helmet commemorating

RAF100, with winners taking part in a flypast over Buckingham Palace.

As I write this (in May 2018) our plans for June are based around our Green badge and its 30th year. Sadly, the many environmental issues raised three decades ago are still a work in progress for today's society, but what has definitely increased is the appetite our

audience has to help the environment – the Green badge is the most popular after the classic Blue. A few years ago we decided to make the *Blue Peter* badges more eco-friendly by making them from recycled yoghurt pots in a factory in Cornwall. This year, to mark the 30th anniversary, we're making a badge out of trees!

Over the summer months ahead, we've got our legendary (dug up 33 years too early…) Millennium Time Capsule on tour across the UK before we send it, together with a brand new for 2018 Diamond Time Capsule, into the National Archives to be safely stored away until the 80th birthday in 2038. We'll be embracing the summer sun with the return of our Sport badge, which current presenter Radzi has designed, and for which our audience have to take up a new sport for at least an hour. So far, in its history, over 60,000 hours of activity have happened thanks to this badge.

As the programme left its longstanding home of BBC Television Centre and moved to MediaCityUK, some might have questioned what its new life in the North would bring to *Blue Peter*, or how successful it might be in the increasing digital age. Well, we now have record amounts of post coming into the programme, increasing every year since 2011, which shows how sending and receiving physical handwritten letters in a digital world is extra special to the children who watch *Blue Peter*. Our replies are still personalised, no letter is the same and the audience really appreciate the direct connection they have with the programme. They love to see their work on screen and their ideas influencing the content we make. Participation is key for *Blue Peter* and we still give exceptional opportunities for our audience to take part in competitions. Tens of thousands applied for the chance to meet Steven Spielberg, go behind the scenes at MI5, create their own animated character with Aardman's Oscar-winning Nick Park, and design one of the best sporting mascots there has ever been, for London 2017 – Hero the Hedgehog. It would be amazing if we could trace back all the *Blue Peter* competition winners to see what happened after the win and what it might have inspired them to do. In 1984, a six-and-a-half-year-old boy won a

competition badge by entering the Liverpool Garden Festival competition and was a top runner-up… I might not be a brilliant gardener, but maybe it did encourage my love of TV…? Yes, that boy was me.

Blue Peter was the first CBBC programme to have its own website and today we still have a very successful digital offering with our popular online fan club, engaging "makes and bakes", exclusive clips from famous celebrities, and entertaining quiz pages. *Blue Peter* is at the heart of

CBBC Buzz (the new app from CBBC) and #bluepeter is always making its mark on every social platform. Being close to the BBC's research and development teams at MediaCityUK, *Blue Peter* will always be at the forefront of technical innovation and digital transformation for BBC Children's with exciting ideas

for the future, so it plays its part in the ambitious BBC Children's "Kids2020" strategy. *Blue Peter* is in great health for a 60-year-old and has a bright future ahead.

After all the planning, I can't wait for the big day in the autumn. *Blue Peter* is a very special club to be part of and the Big Birthday show will be a moment to remember. For the successive production teams who've worked on it, for the editors who've had the pleasure to help shape it – Biddy Baxter, Lewis Bronze, Oliver Macfarlane, Steve Hocking, Richard Marson and Tim Levell – but, most importantly, for its audience, including every lucky badge-holder in the UK who I'm sure will be watching. I hope all generations enjoy reliving their favourite memories, seeing "their" presenters again, but also admire our current team, Lindsey and Radzi, as they fly the flag for *Blue Peter* in 2018.

BEANO'S IMMORTAL BIRTHDAY SECRET!

MICHAEL STIRLING

—

As Beano zooms – Billy Whizz style – towards being 80 years young, it's proud to finally reveal the secret of its success, via a bold call to action: Rebels Wanted! The mission? For us all to think more "kid" and rebel, at least a little, every single day.

National institutions are rarely "rebellious". The definition of the term is not always entirely positive. However, Beano recognises the transformative potential of a rebellious mindset. This everyday rebellion is the recurring factor in Beano's creation, success and enduring appeal.

Beginning as a 28-page comic on 30 July 1938, Beano has since entertained generations.

In late 2016, an exciting multi-media expansion extended the original mission to entertain far beyond the printed form. Beano Studios was created: a global entertainment powerhouse designed to spread the original mischievous magic from the comic worldwide.

At the centre of this

A Beano Studios Product
© D.C. Thomson & Co. Ltd 2018

strategy, beano.com was launched as a new, entirely safe, online playground. A free, daily feed of fun, it's already emulating the original success of the comic, becoming the nation's fastest-growing kids' website.

The weekly comic continues to outperform its market, demonstrating that digital innovation doesn't have to simply replace positive analogue experiences. By avoiding lazy duplication and adopting an iterative, additive approach, Beano is now reaching more fans than ever before.

Over 27 million people in the UK have been regular readers of the comic and a copy is sold every 17 seconds. Digital reach is similarly phenomenal; a recent, good-natured prank upon a famous politician resulted in over three billion online impressions as it enjoyed viral popularity.

It's a virtuous circle of development, inspired by the original rebellious Beano spirit, which advocates taking a chance outside of your natural comfort zone. That something, or someone, can be rebellious and badged "So Beano" has now entered the nation's playground lexicon. It's a badge to be worn with pride. A badge proclaiming "rebel". But what's so great, "So Beano", about rebellion? Is it truly a good thing, or just a cool word?

Simply put, if no one ever rebelled, if we all conformed neatly, it would end innovation, inventions and discovery. Babies are born rebels, brains fizzing with synaptic potential. No concept of restrictive rules and regulations. Behaving instinctively. Spontaneously. Creatively.

Sometimes, this innate ability is nurtured, with awesome results. Leonardo da Vinci was the archetypal childhood rebel, who continued to break rules his entire life. The vast majority of Nobel Prize Winners have been proven to demonstrate rebellious behaviours and attitudes, encouraging them to push things further than most, for positive dividends.

Sadly, potential is more often encumbered, then slowly eroded, via crushing convention. Don't do that! Grow up! Do as I tell you! Stop acting like a seven-year-old! Or worse. Grown-ups rule society. But they're also victims of the tyranny of rules, whether societal conventions, or personal restrictions designed to safeguard self-image, to avoid any risk of embarrassment.

Beano rejects this. Instead, we believe the most important mindset is to think like a kid for ever. To laugh at oneself, every single day. This applies to lapsed kids (i.e. grown-ups) as much as every new generation. So never grow-up: it's a trap!

It seems a simple and positive philosophy but faces strict opposition. In schools, kids who embrace the natural inclination to rebel are stigmatised. They're rewarded for following rules and crushed if they don't. Spirit and creativity is devalued and demotivated. Society therefore loses the opportunity of nurturing minds to provide innovative solutions to the problems we'll face tomorrow. That's a bad thing.

So how do we rebalance a societal disincentive to becoming a rebel? Rebels seem attractive in popular culture – something

BEANO

A Beano Studios Product
© D.C. Thomson & Co. Ltd 2018

dangerous to aspire to, without living such a life ourselves. Beano celebrates thinking differently; more imaginatively. Beano characters show the same attitude in a more conventional and accessible way – anybody could be a rebel. Most importantly, Beano has the provenance and credibility to own this mission.

Historically radical Dundee was the birthplace of Beano, and it was her daughters who powered Beano's rebel heart. At the turn of the last century the city was nicknamed "She Town", due to the high proportion of women who worked in the famous jute mills and their bravery and tenacity in challenging industrial inequality.

A high proportion of these women were the sole family breadwinners – matriarchal figureheads. This created a unique set of circumstances which powered conditions leading to the creation of Beano. Simply, it would never have happened without them.

Dundee's children were inspired by these proud women. They were either mothered by them or worked alongside them. School-aged kids represented the second-largest sector of the jute workforce. Over 20% of Dundee's children held exemption certificates, which meant they spent half their educational hours in factories, developing rebellious attitudes of their own which they could take back and share amongst their classmates.

Women and children were poorly treated in the mills. Despite being the vast majority of the workforce, they were poorly rewarded and factory conditions were appalling. The dangerous environment endured by both their own children and junior co-workers motivated women to actively protest. Unrepresented by formal union support, Dundee's rebel women instead used their own initiative and word-of-mouth organisation. The demand for their labour meant they were confident to rebel against injustice. So, rebel they did. Between 1889 and 1914 there were over 100 recorded strikes led by woman jute workers in one company alone.

The inspirational influence of militant mums and working women upon children cannot be overstated. It's the key reason why Dundee became the epicentre of a national phenomenon in 1911. School strikes!

In an era where the draconian Victorian attitude that "children should be seen, but not heard" was still prevalent, the strikes became a shocking nationwide scandal. Kids all over the UK, increasingly educated and smart enough to read newspapers, were influenced by the potential of industrial action as a lever to improve conditions.

In Dundee, children had first-hand experience of rebellion and the city therefore witnessed the most extensive schoolkid strikes in the country. Less homework and a ban on corporal punishment seemed reasonable demands. Sadly, the rebels were thwarted on this occasion, with even more of the latter the inevitable consequence. However, a rebellious spark had ignited. Pushing back had felt good.

Some of these rebel pupils went on to gain employment in a different sort of factory from their parents – one with infinitely better conditions. This was the Fun Factory at the publisher DC Thomson. It was here that they tore up the rule book of creating comics and used their rebellious spark to make Beano light the way for every generation thereafter.

Print media at that time was hugely influential. Comics for kids were established as a form of entertainment, second only to the movies. Telly was still for posh people – with nothing decent on anyway. It would be a rebellious move to dare to change the existing, successful comic formula. Challenge accepted!

The standard text-heavy adventure stories were jettisoned, replaced with a rebellious new approach. A cheeky sense of humour was combined with a determination to tell stories visually above everything else. Critics were stunned by DC Thomson sanctioning what they snobbishly – and mistakenly – viewed as an intellectually inferior product.

The new format ultimately made Beano more accessible, inviting ever more recruits into a world of mischief and mayhem. The fact that they were often showing up the adult world was even more rebellious!

This rebellion was emphasised by brave, continued production during the war years. Overcoming paper shortages, Beano fulfilled a secret mission to affect a propaganda battle against the enemy. The consequence of this was the chilling post-war discovery of a Nazi-hit list which marked Beano staff for the ultimate sanction.

The rebellious momentum of thinking kids continued after the war via another notable innovation. During the '50s, Beano's character cast was revolutionised to focus upon kids as the heroes. This focus was again deemed rebellious – especially when the majority of the stories had the kids not fighting against one another, but uniting to question and usurp adult authority.

Cover star Biffo the Bear – inspired by the transatlantic success of Mickey Mouse (resembling a more hard-bitten creature who'd endured a far tougher paper round) – was upstaged by Dennis, Minnie, Rodger and the Bash Street Kids. Beano was now entirely ruled by rebellious kids, and has been ever since.

The characters – and the Beano fans they represent – remain indefatigably mischievous, always prepared to take every situation to the limit. Wantonly outrageous behaviour is morally smacked-down by a justifiable twist of fate. The inspirational truth is, no matter how many times our characters are toppled, they demonstrate a resilient "bouncebackability" to rebel yet again.

Today, the world needs Beano as a rebel's reference guide more than ever. Kids are questioning prime ministers and presidents; bombing and Brexit. Beano knows this due to the extensive audience insight which informs everything we create and do. A rebellious kid is more likely to discover the cure for illness or become a transformative entrepreneur. These heroes of the future will be So Beano!

Beano exists to remind us that we can all be everyday rebels in some small yet important way. We should always search for the rebel inside ourselves. No matter what age we reach, by thinking like kids we can feel forever young. Once a rebel, always a rebel.

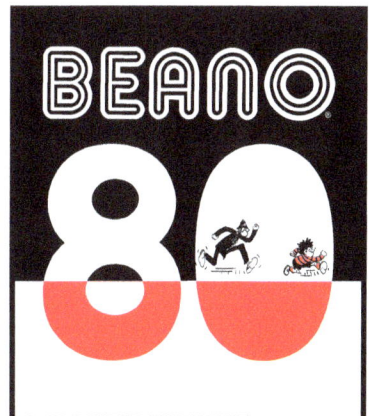

TRIBUTE TO BRIAN CANT

JONATHAN COHEN

Photos: Paul R Jackson collection

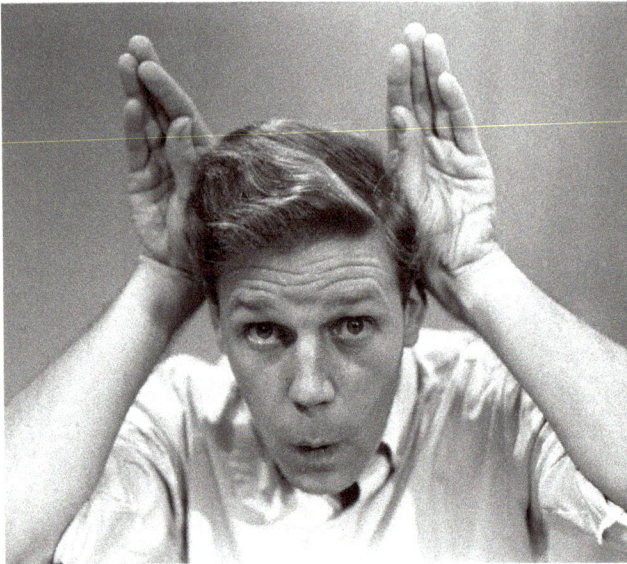

I am so privileged and fortunate to have had the legend that is Brian Cant as a dear and close friend. He was generous and kind, both off and on stage and would never upstage or hog the limelight; in fact, he would be pushing you forward and encouraging you to give your best, such was his lack of ego. His delivery to camera in children's television programmes such as *Play School* and *Play Away* was nothing short of genius, every child watching at home feeling he was addressing them personally.

I have such fond and happy memories of our two man shows which we toured round the country with Brian in the driver's seat, along with our director Cherry, his wife, and their dog Colonel, a bouncy wire haired fox terrier who ate my shoes and make-up sponge and would perform with us on stage. Brian's gift for comedy and observation allowed him to become many wonderful zany characters; Groucho Marx at one point, and a ridiculous Hungarian magician called Heinz Beanz who got everything wrong and would insult me, much to the delight of our young (and old) audiences. He was my friend and will be hugely missed; a trouper in the best sense of the word and a great loss to the world of entertainment.

TRIBUTE TO EMMA TENNANT

LUCY GOODMAN

—

Ten years ago, I nervously sat down clutching materials, a laptop and earphones at an abandoned lunch table on the first floor of the New York Hilton Hotel to meet CiTV's then digital channels and children's controller, Emma Tennant, for the first time.

Having produced children's shows for various other companies, this time I was pitching my own show on behalf of my own brand new indie, and was quite frankly terrified.

Although already in discussion with one broadcaster, I'd heard through the grapevine that CiTV, who up to that point had only been acquiring, might just be looking at commissioning again – so I picked up the phone.

"I'm afraid Emma's diary is jammed for the next two months," her assistant ruefully told me, but just as I was scrolling through towards the May page of my calendar, she added, "Unless of course you're in New York for Kidscreen next week?" My finger stopped abruptly at April. "Yes!" I squeaked "I so am!"

I so wasn't! But having hastily found a flight I wondered, as I checked in to the grottiest hotel ever – you know, the bathroom down the corridor, the dodgy looking permanent resident kind of hotel – what on earth possessed me to come all this way for one meeting.

But in that dusty conference corner, I wrapped up the pitch and held my breath. Emma was very quiet. Thoughtful. I began packing materials. "Yes I like it. I like it a lot," Emma said. "What was the budget again?"

Darn it but I hate that question and eyes down I prepared for the builder-type sharp intake of breath that usually followed my answer. She scribbled in her pad for torturous seconds. "Yup I'll take it – love it, thank you, gotta go. Talk in London. Bye!" With that she disappeared back into the hustle and bustle of a hundred other pitching producers and within ten weeks we were in pre-production. And so *Bookaboo*, the rock puppy with an unquenchable thirst for picture books, was born.

So too was a gratitude, a fondness and respect for one of the most decisive, bold and gracious commissioners I know. In fact, if you could write a description of a producer's perfect broadcaster, you'd write a description of Emma Tennant. There were no airs or graces. She was responsive, grounded, warm, supportive, instinctive, brave, a risk taker, quirky and so trusting of those working around her. Not a single micro-management fibre to be found!

And sixteen months later, whilst we sat clutching each other's hands as the BAFTA nominations were read out, I whispered a "Thank you, Emma." "No, thank you," she whispered back before our names were read out and off to the stage I floated for the first of the many awards that were to follow.

I'm not alone in being hugely privileged to have worked with Emma. The impact and legacy of her time in the children's industry is there for many of us today. We miss her as a work colleague and we miss her as a friend.

RIP Emma Tennant.

CONTRIBUTORS

CONTRIBUTORS

Bob Ayres

Bob Ayres is a BAFTA-winning producer and writer. He runs TrueTube, a charity-funded website for schools which makes short films to help young people reflect on moral, social and religious issues. Bob was a teacher for 15 years, working in Kenya, Birmingham and East London before joining TrueTube in 2010. Originally employed as an education writer, he rose through the ranks to seize editorial control of the site, and now wields his power like a mighty sword. In 2017, TrueTube became the first ever online-only platform to win the Children's BAFTA for Channel of the Year.

Kay Benbow

Kay Benbow was the CBeebies controller from 2010 to 2017. She commissioned all content – TV, online, apps and radio, for the BBC's pre-school channel. Under Kay's leadership, CBeebies became a multi-genre, multi-platform offering. This much loved and most watched children's channel was awarded BAFTA Children's Channel of the Year four times during Kay's tenure. With over 25 years of experience in children's programming, Kay is now an independent consultant and remains passionate about providing the very best content for the youngest audience. Kay@kaybenbow.com.

Will Brenton

Will Brenton has co-created, written, produced and directed some of today's best known programmes for children, including *The Tweenies* (BBC), *Jim Jam and Sunny* (ITV), *Boo!* (BBC), *Fun Song Factory* (GMTV, ITV), *BB3B* (CBBC), *Wibbly Pig* (BBC), *Mighty-Mites* (BBC), *Florrie's Dragons* (Disney), *Melody* (BBC) and *Wanda and the Alie*n (C5/Nick Jr). He is currently co-directing and show running *Team Jay for Juventus*, and *Dive in and Do It* for Sky Television. Later this year he will be returning to *Emmerdale* to direct, followed by *Eastenders*. Will's live shows include 26 arena tours such as *The Tweenies*, *Bob the Builder*, *Thomas the Tank Engine*, *Doctor Who: The Monsters are Coming!* and *The Tale of Mr Tumble* for the Manchester International Festival/Cbeebies.

Chloe Bartlem

Chloe Bartlem is a qualitative senior research executive and works alongside Lesley Salem on Razor Kids. Prior to working in research, Chloe worked in media and advertising, understanding audience demographics to develop impactful communications. Chloe loves working with kids and young people and has experience of this in both research, and from previous roles in mentor and leadership programmes.

Howard Blumenthal

Howard Blumenthal created and produced PBS's *Where in the World is Carmen Sandiego*? in the US and elsewhere. He continues the global citizenship tradition with Kids on Earth (www.kidsonearth.org), interviewing children and teenagers around the world. He has developed and produced shows for Cartoon Network, History, Food Network, Nickelodeon, MTV, FX and more and is a former Bertelsmann and Hearst senior executive. Howard is currently a visiting scholar at he University of Pennsylvania and is also the author of 20+ books. He often confuses work with play.

Anna Campbell

Anna Campbell has over 20 years' experience in research, with a focus on consumer behaviour and digital strategy. She has designed and delivered complex and innovative research projects across a wide range of sectors, nationally and internationally. She also specialises in understanding how children and young people use digital media, and the dynamics of digital behaviour within the home. Recently this has included investigating how voice technology is changing children's engagement with media and brands. Before joining Sparkler as a partner, Anna ran her own boutique digital research agency for 15 years.

Greg Childs

Greg Childs worked for over 25 years at the BBC, mainly as a director, producer and executive producer of children's programmes. He created the first Children's BBC websites and, as head of children's digital, developed and launched the children's channels, CBBC and CBeebies. Greg left the BBC in 2004 and advised producers on digital, interactive and cross-platform strategies, and broadcasters on channel launches, digital futures and management support. He was in the launch teams for Teachers TV and the CITV Channel in the UK, and was advisor to the Al Jazeera Children's Channel for three years. He also consulted with the European Broadcasting Union on their Children's and Youth strategy. As editorial director of the Children's Media Conference, Greg has grown this annual event into a gathering of 1,200+ delegates, with over 200 speakers, and spin-off events and activities year-round. He is also one of the heads of studies at the German Akademie für Kindermedien, and director of the Children's Media Foundation.

Jonathan Cohen

Jonathan Cohen won a scholarship to the Royal Academy of Music where he became a Fellow of the Royal College of Organists and won the Royal Over-Seas League medal for accompaniment. He is perhaps best known for his work in television. He was the musical director for the children's programme *Play Away* and for many years he worked on *Play School* and *Jackanory* and presented the BBC Schools programme *Music Time*. Jonathan also composed the music for many television programmes including the ever popular *Come Outside*. He has presented and conducted concerts with the London Symphony Orchestra both at the Barbican Centre and in America and every Christmas he presents his Christmas Carol Singalong at the Royal Albert Hall.

Phil Dobree

Phil Dobree is the founder of Jellyfish Pictures. He has worked in all genres of content creation including film, commercials, animation, games and broadcast TV, winning multiple BAFTA, VES, RTS and EMMY awards. Phil has a unique insight into the industry after running Jellyfish and helping it grow into one of the most respected VFX and animation companies in the world with a staff of 200. He has assisted the company in pioneering cloud technology, resulting in seamless hybrid rendering solutions and the creation of "virtual studios". He has helped bring in and overseen work from leading studios and broadcasters including *Star Wars: Rogue One* and *Star Wars: The Last Jedi* in film; to *Outlander*, *Black Mirror*, *Dennis and Gnasher: Unleashed*, *Bitz and Bob* and *Floogals* for TV in just the last two years. Phil is also a BAFTA, RTS and VES judge and a member of the VFX/digital effects and animation chapter of BAFTA. He sits on the board of UK Screen Alliance, Animation UK and the council of the Creative Industries Federation. He was selected as one of the RTS Broadcast HOT 100 most influential people in Broadcast Media in 2012/13.

Helen Dugdale

Helen Dugdale is a Manchester-based author, journalist and PR consultant and founder of Scribble, the PR and content agency. She has over 20 years' worth of national and international experience promoting and writing for events and brands aimed at children and families. Helen writes for a range of global platforms, contributing interviews and editorials on media literacy for primary school children to A-level students. She established Deckchair Adventures in April 2018, an educational travel website that offers stories and reviews helping children learn more about the cities and countries they visit on holiday through literature, film, TV and music.

Lucy Goodman

Lucy Goodman has over twenty years' experience in the television industry in both Australia and the UK as a creator/ writer/producer/director. She formed Happy Films to produce stand-out quality children's and family media. With a slew of awards including two BAFTA wins, a Prix Jeunesse and five Emmy nominations for *Bookaboo*, the pre-school show she created, Lucy thrives on creating fun and meaningful content with heart. Prior to forming Happy Films, Lucy headed up children's for Alibi Productions and earned Disney Junior UK its first BAFTA nomination. She has made programmes for BBC, BBC Schools, ITV, Disney and Nickelodeon.

Diana Hinshelwood

Diana Hinshelwood started her television career in children's TV as a production secretary on *Record Breakers*, followed by *Grange Hill* – two iconic BBC Children's programmes. She has worked in children's media for over 30 years on well-known children's programmes such as *Going Live* and *Playdays*. Diana joined CBeebies as a producer at the launch of the channel. As a freelance producer, she has worked on *LazyTown*, *Sarah and Duck* and *The Fluffy Club*. She has also begun producing for digital platforms and has worked as a development producer, winning option agreements

for animations and a commission for CBeebies Radio.

Anna Home OBE

Anna Home OBE began working for the BBC in 1960 and started working in the children's department in 1964. She has won many accolades including a BAFTA lifetime achievement award. She was the first chair of the BAFTA Children's Committee, has chaired both the EBU Children's and Youth Working Group and the Prix Jeunesse International Advisory Board. Anna was the Chair of the Save Kids' TV Campaign Executive Committee and the Showcomotion Children's Media Conference. She now chairs the boards of the Children'Media Conferene and the Children's Media Foundation and is a board member of Screen South.

Cato Hunt

Cato Hunt is the director of Space Doctors. She has spent her career helping clients grow the cultural impact of their brands through a deep understanding of changing cultural meaning. Using hybrid, experimental approaches fusing semiotics with other disciplines, Cato pioneers new ways for brands to understand, measure and create meaning – from the stories they tell to the experiences they deliver. With an MBA thesis on the marketing of character merchandise to children, she is passionate about finding new ways

in which brands can catalyse positive cultural change.

Chris Jarvis

Chris Jarvis is best known for his work on BBC Children's, hosting *The Broom Cupboard* from 1993 and then fronting a variety of shows including *Fully Booked*, *The Friday Zone*, *Look Sharp*, *Playdays*, *Jungle Run*, *Dream Street* and *Step Inside*. He wrote CBBC's first soap opera, *Wood Lane TV*, about a shambolic television station with Chris and Josie d'Arby playing all the characters. In 2002, Chris helped launch CBeebies with Pui Fan Lee; they hit it off as friends and remained a double act ever since. In 2009, they co-devised and hosted *Show Me Show Me*, packed with songs, comedy sketches and imaginative play. Now in its seventh series, it is shown twice a day, every day for most of the year. They also dreamt up the multi-award-winning *Old Jack's Boat*, starring Bernard Cribbins. Chris has written, starred in and directed dozens of pantomimes on TV, radio and the UK's finest theatres including eight in Bournemouth and four in Richmond. This year you'll find him giving his Dick (Whittington) at the Lighthouse in Poole. Twitter: @realchrisjarvis

Kayleigh Keam

Kayleigh Keam writes and directs for CBeebies as an assistant producer. She has five years' experience writing and producing audio series for the under-six age group on CBeebies Radio, including *The Furchester Hotel*, *Something Special*, *Tree Fu Tom* and *Do You Know?* Kayleigh began her career as a broadcast assistant at BBC Radio Norfolk and Cambridgeshire. In 2017, she went part-time to pursue her writing career and is writing a children's book for 8–12-year-olds.

John Kent

John Kent is an award-winning digital executive and strategist who has been working at the forefront of digital innovation for more than 20 years. As a former executive at the BBC and head of digital at Kids Industries, he's led the successful digital transformation of some of the biggest brands in kids – including CBeebies, Peppa and the Al Jazeera's children's channels. More recently he's been working as a consultant, helping brands and blue chip businesses use digital to better connect with audiences through digital engagement. John is a regular contributor to the Children's Media Conference, and an active member of the Children's Media Foundation where he leads on digital policy and tech matters relating to children.

Terri Langan

Terri Langan started creating children's content in 2011, after 15 years working as a producer in sport, all factual genres and as head of development for indies in London and Manchester. After having her twin boys and becoming increasingly absorbed in the programmes they watched, Terri joined BBC Children's in 2011 and, for almost four years, led the CBeebies in-house development team, where her commissions included BAFTA-winning *Old Jack's Boat*, *Swashbuckle*, RTS-award-winning *CBeebies Stargazing* and *Biggleton*. She joined Hello Halo in 2017 as executive producer after creating brand new CBeebies series *Junk Rescue* and wouldn't leave! So, she now heads up their children's department where she spends her days watching kids' TV, reading kids' books and playing kids' games, all in the name of research.

Allanah Langstaff

Allanah Langstaff is an experienced producer working in development and production across a range of genres and channels including children's, daytime and factual entertainment. She most recently served as producer on Hello Halo's first series for CBeebies, *Junk Rescue*, and has recently finished a stint on a new Stacey Dooley Documentary for BBC1 primetime. She is currently working in development at Hungry Bear and previously honed her passion for popular factual as part of the inaugural team at indie Hello Halo, STV Productions, the BBC and Maverick TV.

David Levine

David Levine is vice president, programming, production and strategic development, Disney Channels EMEA, and general manager, Disney Channels UK & Ireland, Nordics. As vice president, he is responsible for all strategic and operational aspects of programming across Disney Channels EMEA, including the development of the linear and multi-platform programming strategy. David is responsible for the direction of original production and overseeing the development and production slates of originally produced content, acquisitions and co-productions. His team is responsible for developing and commissioning innovative and tailored content that listens to what kids want. Recent successes include the Disney Channel's ratings hit *The Lodge*, web comedy *So Sammy* created by Miranda Hart, written by Rob Evans and produced by Jo Sargent, and *First Class Chefs: Family Style* presented by Matt Tebbutt and Gia Ré. As general manager of Disney Channels UK & Ireland, Nordics, David leads a team that utilises these key platforms to drive familiarity and awareness for the Disney brand and content, through key partnerships with Sky Broadcasting, Virgin Media and more. David joined Disney in March 2004, serving multiple roles in US programming, worldwide programming and Channel GM. Prior to Disney, David worked for Ragdoll USA as Vice President Business Affairs and Development. David also serves as the executive sponsor for Pride UK & Ireland, Disney's first-ever international LGBT resource group, providing guidance and support for the team.

Estelle Lloyd

Estelle Lloyd is co-founder of Azoomee, the kids' digital TV and game app available on tablets, smartphones and connected TVs. Available in over 40 countries, the app includes games, videos and messaging to have fun and learn in a safe and ad-free environment. Parents love the simplicity, value for money and peace of mind it offers: it's safe, free from advertising or in-app purchases, the content is curated by humans (not algorithms) and it has some learning games and videos too. Sold as a family subscription in app stores and by B2B2C partners including O2, Argos, Amazon and Vodafone, Azoomee is supported by the NSPCC, one of the world's leading children's charities. Estelle has spent her whole career in media and technology, starting in New York working in the tech and media investment banking industry for ten years. In 2006, Estelle founded her first start-up in digital publishing, sold to FTSE 250 Centaur Media plc in 2011. As one of the UK's leading female technology entrepreneurs, Estelle is an experienced public speaker and press interviewer on the subjects of financing entrepreneurial businesses, building and scaling a tech business and mobile and technology trends. As a strong supporter of women-led businesses, she is also an investor and non-executive board director to several start-ups.

Anna Mansi

Anna Mansi is head of certification at the British Film Institute. She works closely with key stakeholders in government and across the screen sectors to provide advice and guidance on the application processes for all of the cultural tests, co-production treaties and policies relating to all of the creative sector tax reliefs, including film, high-end television, animation television, children's television and video games.

Anna regularly speaks on panels at conferences and events to promote the tax reliefs such as the Children's Media Conference, the Develop Games conference and many others. In addition, Anna has organised BFI-led seminars and events for the animation, video games and children's television sectors.

Alex Milne Turner

Alex Milne Turner is an analyst at MTM, with recent experience leading projects for the BBC and Discovery. Alongside studying philosophy, politics, and economics, Alex produced lots of theatre at university – including a shambolic children's focused adaptation of *Tintin*. He enjoys exploring new technological developments, including AI and machine learning, and would love to discuss any of the above (just don't ask him to perform *Tintin*).

Alison Norrington

Alison Norrington is a writer/producer and founder of storycentral, developing groundbreaking properties with global partners in film, television, animation, publishing, advertising, theme parks, VR and gaming. She specialises in story-telling and engagement, experience design, franchise extension and development. Alison is also a bestselling novelist, playwright, journalist and a PhD researcher. She is conference chair for StoryWorld Conference, executive

producer of the Children's Media Conference VR thread and a two-time TEDx speaker. She is a featured BAFTA Guru and a member of the International Academy of Television Arts & Sciences, Themed Entertainment Association, The Writers Guild of Great Britain and Women in Film & TV. www.storycentral.com @storycentral

Tom O'Connell

Tom O'Connell is a north-based television writer, producer and director. Tom is currently series producing *The Baby Club*, a Three Arrows Production for CBeebies. Last year Tom produced *Treasure Champs* – also for Three Arrows – and has been involved with children's productions including *Marrying Mum and Dad*, *The Let's Go Club*, *Mr Bloom: Here and There*, *CBeebies Stargazing* and *Swashbuckle*. Tom has produced content for BBC Learning and BBC Teach, working with brands such as *Stargazing LIVE*, *Britain in a Day* and the BBC Philharmonic. Tom lives in Ramsbottom with his partner, Eve, and their children.

Beth Parker

Beth Parker joined Disney in 2014 to look after the production of animated content for Disney channels across the EMEA region. Over the last twenty years, she has worn a number of different hats: running a studio, head of production for an international brand management company, freelance producer and social entrepreneur. Beth speaks a handful of languages and holds two masters degrees, in music, and in criminology. She has been the Animation Chair of Animated Women UK since October 2017.

Ed Petrie

Ed Petrie currently presents CBBC's *Marrying Mum and Dad* and *All Over the Place*, which are on their seventh and ninth series respectively. He was the main continuity presenter on CBBC for three years with his cactus sidekick Oucho, and his past shows include *Ed and Oucho's Excellent Inventions* and *Transmission Impossible with Ed and Oucho*, as well as frequent appearances on other CBBC programmes. He began performing stand-up in 2002 and started regularly presenting and acting in children's television on Nickelodeon from 2005, before moving to CBBC in 2007. Twitter: edpetrie
Instagram: officialedpetrie

Andy Phippen

Andy Phippen is professor of children and technology at Plymouth University. He has specialised in the use of ICT by children and young people for over 15 years, carrying out a large amount of grass roots research on issues such as their attitudes toward privacy and data protection, internet safety and contemporary issues such as sexting, peer abuse and the impact of digital technology on children's wellbeing. He has presented written and oral evidence to parliamentary inquiries related to the children's use of ICT and is widely published in the area.

Gary Pope

Gary Pope is co-founder of Kids Industries, a company that makes family brands stronger. Gary began his career as a school teacher before becoming a learning designer for a change management consultancy. Today Gary leads Kids Industries, solving problems, developing strategies and creating content for brands as diverse as Kellogg, Peppa Pig and Al Jazeera. The company undertakes research and strategy and makes everything from new ranges of toothpastes to entirely new TV channels, complete with SVOD capabilities. Gary is a school governor, dad, uncle, great uncle, godfather and LEGO collector.

Nigel Pope

Nigel Pope is a producer specialising in children's and natural history programming. Creator of *Raven*, *Springwatch* and *Gudrun the Viking Princess*, Nigel also produced *Big Cat Week*, *The Really Wild Show* and many other shows and formats both in-house at Bristol's world-renowned BBC Natural History Unit, and more recently as an independent producer. In 2010, Nigel set up Maramedia with Jackie Savery, now a leading Scottish independent production company creating content for the BBC, PBS, National Geographic, CBBC and Cbeebies. Maramedia's central mission is to create content with a life beyond television, working alongside wildlife NGOs and reconnecting children with the natural world. Nigel and Maramedia have won or been nominated for BAFTA, RTS, Wildscreen PANDA and Prime-time Emmy awards.

Nick Richardson

Nick Richardson is the founder of award-winning research agency, The Insights People. Nick has set out to change the way in which global market research is conducted, allowing clients to make informed decisions and develop strategies built on quality insight, niche market segmentation and real-time data. Through its Kids Insights and Parents Insights service, The Insights People surveys 800 different children every single week in both the UK and USA and a further 200 parents in the UK. With over 300,000 data points added into its online portal on a weekly basis and insight-led reports issued every 12 weeks, The Insights People offers the most comprehensive and up-to-date resource available. kidsinsights.co.uk/yearbook.

Naomi Sakr

Naomi Sakr is professor of media policy at the Communication and Media Research Institute (CAMRI), University of Westminster. From 2013 to 2016 she led research into children's screen content in the Arab region, funded by the Arts and Humanities Research Council (AHRC), and in 2017–18 worked on another AHRC-funded project exploring approaches to diversifying European children's screen content in the wake of recent forced migration from Syria, Iraq and other parts of the Middle East, captured in a series of briefings based on workshops held in Manchester, Copenhagen and Munich. She has written books on Arab television and journalism in Egypt and edited volumes of research on women and media, media and politics, and media moguls in the Middle East. She co-edited *Children's TV and Digital Media in the Arab World: Childhood, Screen Culture and Education* with Jeanette Steemers (2017) and is co-authoring a book with her on Arab-European encounters in the field of children's screen content.

Lesley Salem

Lesley Salem heads up Razor Kids, a specialist family unit at Razor Research. Razor Research already has a track record in helping brands grow and Razor Kids applies the very same strategic rigour and commercial acumen when talking to children and their families and teasing out insights. As well as being a mum of three teens, Lesley has worked with children, youths and families for over two decades, across several marketing disciplines – innovation, trends and qualitative research. Lesley is restless in finding new ways to extract rich insights and help younger audiences respond to conceptual ideas and stimulus in a meaningful and appropriate way. She also finds ways to integrate child psychology, educational and sociology models to aid analysis. Her work has taken her all over the world, working with various media and entertainment brands, as well as FMCG and retail clients.

Angela Salt

Angela Salt is a content creator, writer and development & creative consultant. She is the founder of Salt Content, which launches at the 2018 Children's Media Conference. She is currently writing for several international animated TV shows for children including *Curious George* (NBCUniversal Animation, USA); *Krash and Hehe* (Sino-Russian co-production for CCTV produced by Fun Union, HK) and *The Curious World of Linda* (Taktoon, S.Korea for KBS). Angela has written the pilot for a new children's series, *Streetcat Bob*, based on the real-life hero cat turned book and movie-star, animated by King Rollo Films.

Colette Sensier

Colette Sensier is project executive at Space Doctors. As part of Space Doctors' Insight team, she uses semiotic and cultural analysis to uncover new stories about cultures, sectors and rapidly shifting attitudes. She joined Space Doctors in 2017 after spending several years as a freelance analyst, copywriter and journalist, and enjoys incorporating diverse disciplines and voices into her work. Colette holds a BA in English from Cambridge, an MA in Creative Writing from UEA, and published a book of poetry with Eyewear Press in 2014.

Kath Shackleton

Kath Shackleton is producer at Fettle Animation, a twice BAFTA-nominated animation production company in Pennine Yorkshire. Fettle is a service studio, making animation for broadcast, education, businesses and charities. Fettle's animated series made with BBC Learning, based on accounts of Holocaust survivors, won a Japan Prize, a Sandford St Martin Award and two Royal Television Society Awards. It has been broadcast in 12 countries and made into a graphic novel.

Christine Singer

Christine Singer is a post-doctoral research associate in the Department of Culture, Media, and Creative Industries, King's College London, where she is working on the AHRC-funded project "Children's Screen Content in an Era of Forced Migration: Facilitating Arab-European Dialogue". She holds a PhD in Media Studies from SOAS, University of London, with her doctoral thesis exploring notions of childhood and coming of age in relation to film, television, and digital screen media in post-apartheid South Africa.

Professor Jeanette Steemers

Professor Jeanette Steemers is Professor of Culture, Media and Creative Industries at King's College London. After working for research company, CIT Research, and international television distributor HIT Entertainment, she rejoined academia in 1993. She has published widely on international distribution, public service broadcasting and the children's media industry including *Selling Television* (2004), *European Television Industries* (2005 with P. Iosifidis and M. Wheeler), *Creating Preschool Television* (2010), *The Media and the State* (2016 with T. Flew and P. Iosifidis), *European Media in Crisis* (2015 with J. Trappel and B. Thomass) and *Children's TV and Digital Media in the Arab World* (2017 with Naomi Sakr). Her work has

been funded by the British Academy, the Leverhulme Trust and the Arts and Humanities Research Council. She is currently working on an AHRC project that seeks to facilitate Arab-European dialogue on children's screen content in an era of forced migration.

Michael Stirling

Michael Stirling is head of Beano Studios, Scotland. Since July 2016, he has undertaken a creative and commercial role across publishing, digital and consumer divisions. Prior to this, Michael became Editor-in-Chief of the *Beano* in 2010, a job he described as the "ultimate" job in journalism. During his tenure he established the *Beano* as the number one Christmas Annual and grew the subscriber base by over 480%. In 2007, he added editorial responsibility for DC Thomson's iconic boys› titles, including the *Beano*, the *Dandy*, *Commando*, *The Broons* and *Oor Wullie* Michael successfully launched DC Thomson titles *WWE Kids* and *110% Gaming*, and worked on the BAFTA-nominated hit international TV animation, *Dennis & Gnasher*. Previously he was celebrity editor on *Shout* magazine, before progressing to become deputy editor of the UK's bestselling teen title.

Anna Taylor

Anna Taylor is a researcher at Fundamentally Children, where she

supports app and toy companies with parent and child market research, including focus groups and product testing. Her notable projects include ongoing user testing of the McDonald's Happy Studio app, and the development of an evidence-based "Toys as the Tools of Play" benefit framework for the British Toy and Hobby Association. Anna is a Psychology BSc graduate and shares Fundamentally Children's passion for promoting childhood learning and development through play. Anna.taylor@fundamentallychildren. com www.FundamentallyChildrenHQ. com

Ewan Vinnicombe

Ewan Vinnicombe has been the editor of *Blue Peter* since 2013 and has the overall responsibility and creative control for the brand on TV and digital. Ewan has said that it's the best job he's had whilst working in BBC Children's for nearly 20 years. He loves reading all the correspondence from the audience which helps him to develop his ideas for the content for *Blue Peter*. Ewan has worked on other key children's content including *Springwatch Trackers*, Saturday morning TV, *Record Breakers* and was the head of presentation responsible for CBBC HQ and CBeebies House content including *Bedtime Stories*. Ewan was awarded his Blue Peter badge when he was six for being a top runner-up in the *Blue Peter* Liverpool Garden Festival competition in 1984.

The Children's Media
FOUNDATION

www.ingramcontent.com/pod-product-compliance
Lightning Source LLC
Chambersburg PA
CBHW051559030426
42334CB00031B/3259